EX LIBRIS
TSM

The View from Here

Also by Robert M. Coates

Eater of Darkness

The Outlaw Years

Yesterday's Burdens

All the Year Round

Bitter Season

Wisteria Cottage

The Farther Shore

The Hour after Westerly

The View from Here

by Robert M. Coates

Harcourt, Brace and Company · New York

To my son, Tony

The View from Here

 **one**

Largely because we moved about so much, and therefore developed few really intimate friendships anywhere, my family had, I think—there were only the three of us: my mother, my father, and myself—a rather closer relationship than most. We did move about, all right. My father started as a machinist, as his own father and grandfather had done before him. But he wound up functioning alternately as a part-time inventor and a designer of special machinery—in a sense, an embryonic form of what then hadn't yet been christened an "efficiency engineer"—and his work in the latter capacity took him, and us, variously, to Rochester, Buffalo, Seattle, Cincinnati, New York, and other way stops, for stays ranging from a few months up to two or three years, depending on his mood and his commitments.

Once, even, he hauled us all the way out to Colorado, while he had a whack at gold mining. But I believe I'll save the full account of our wanderings for another chapter. One result of it, at any rate, was that everywhere we went, I was, for a period at least, the new boy, the outsider. I didn't resent it particularly then and I still don't, though

I've been told by more psychologically minded acquaintances that the experience must have scarred me for keeps. That was just the way life *was*, I thought, and while it did make for stretches of loneliness and uncertainty, it had its excitements, too. Though I never thought of it at the time, I can see now that my parents, as well, must have been a little bit out of things frequently.

As I say, I didn't notice it then. (A boy, after all, pays little real attention to his parents' problems; parents are just *there*.) And my father was very gregarious. He was always striking up conversations with strangers and bringing business friends home unexpectedly for dinner, and though my mother felt obligated to complain occasionally, she really enjoyed it, for she, too, liked company.

In their turn, they were invited out fairly frequently, or so it seemed to me; and my mother, whenever we stayed put anywhere long enough to get sufficiently involved in the local doings, was an ardent club-woman—and in an era when too much activity of that sort on the part of a woman was regarded with some suspicion; it made her seem like a suffragette, which, in fact, she also was. While we lived in Rochester, I remember, at around the time of the Vernon Castles and the beginning of the great vogue for dancing, she and my father joined one of the dancing clubs that were springing up everywhere. They went out to it every Thursday evening, my father dressed in his best and my mother looking her prettiest, to practice the intricacies of the one-step, the tango, and the maxixe. When they came home, still exhilarated, they often put a record on the Victrola and started all over again (one, two, pause, step, pivot, and so on) while I watched, I'm afraid a trifle disdainfully. I was still at the age when I considered dancing a device invented by girls to contribute to the discomfiture of boys.

No, I don't want to give the impression that our home life, ever or anywhere, was bleak or depressing. Yet I can see now that underneath it all there was a certain loneliness on their part, too. The friends they made were friends, so to speak, of passage, and I can remember now that my mother often recalled rather wistfully their early days in New Haven, where she and my father had grown up, met, and married, and where, as she put it, they had "known just about everybody"; and—perhaps the surest proof of her need to maintain some feeling of continuity—she kept up what was in the end a truly massive correspondence, writing regularly to people she had not seen in years, but whom she had met, and remembered fondly, along our way.

The result of all this, though, was to bind us more closely together; there were no barriers between me and my parents, and surely this was a compensation. We had our private jokes and private references—after all, why wouldn't we, when we had journeyed together from New England to Portland and Seattle and back again, and had shared all sorts of intimate adventures along the way? If others looked blank at hearing some of them, we did not care. We felt defiant. We were the traveled ones, the will-o'-the-wisps, the gypsies; they were the stay-at-homes, and if we insisted on that difference—possibly, as I think of it now, a trifle too much—that didn't matter greatly, either; it only emphasized our own compactness.

The fact was, we *liked* being together. We played games together—hearts, crokinole, parcheesi; simple games like that—on the living-room table; or my father and mother would play cribbage or whist while I did my homework across the table from them, but under the same dome-shaped, colored-glass hanging lamp that was one of the standard articles of furniture of the time, and in the same warm, enfolding atmosphere.

Oddly, though, my own sense of continuity depends in great part on the thinnest thread of all—a mere whistled phrase of music that was our family "call." It was our way of signaling to one another, in a crowd or on the street or elsewhere, and I don't suppose many people go in for that sort of thing nowadays; I imagine the very noise of the traffic would defeat it. But, like the sound of those personal motifs in Wagner, heralding Tristan, or Wotan, or the Valkyrie, it still, after all these years, means "family" to me.

Our call was simple enough, certainly. To produce it, you just puckered up your lips and, starting around middle C, ran up swiftly to as high a note as you could conveniently whistle, and then trailed back down in a slow, slow, slow glissando, ending about where you had started. But the effect of the swift, darting rise and the slow descent always had, and still has, for me a certain poignance. It was like the rapid rise and dead fall of a rocket (here I mean an innocent, early-time Fourth of July rocket, not the intercontinental kind), and perhaps because of this mixture of qualities that it had, the memories it brings back are mixed, too, half exultant and half wistful.

For one thing, my father, in his ebullience, always let loose a blast or two, like a steamer approaching its harbor, as he came home in the evening from his shop or his office to wherever we happened to be living at the moment; and so the slight mournfulness of dusk and day's ending is associated with it, as well as a varied feeling of *place*—of, for instance, the planked sidewalks and steep, rutted roadway of South Fourth Street in Victor, Colorado, where we lived in my father's gold-mining phase (and the great sprawl of the Portland Mine, halfway up Bull Mountain, at the head of it and dominating the town); of the even steeper and shabbier streets of Independence (not far from Victor and nearer my father's mine, but still in the Victor and Cripple Creek district; we lived there only briefly, for it was a tough little settlement and my mother didn't like it); of the neatly shrubbed, wide-lawned, shaded expanse of Humboldt Parkway in Buffalo (we had come east by then, and had prospered).

I hear the sound of it, and again it is twilight, coming up from the trolley stop on Dewey Avenue at the foot of the playground of P.S. 7 in Rochester. I was in high school by then, and P.S. 7 was only a grade school. But it had a tennis court, and tennis was our passion at the period; we older kids would play until, literally, it was so dark that the only way a fellow could see the ball was by keeping his eyes fixed unremittingly upon it; if he looked away even for a moment, it was lost to view irrevocably in the darkness. But we played on and on—Bill Lakeman, Charley Keeley, Ted Benedict, others—trying desperately to prolong the pleasures of the moment and delay their passing, until something or someone stopped us. In my case, it was usually the sound of our call. There was a row of little shops down there at the trolley stop, all of them with their windows lighted at that time of day; barely distinguishable in the gathering darkness, there would also be the figure of my father, just alighted from the trolley on his way home from his machine shop on State Street, and whistling for me. And I would know that halfway down the block behind, on Bryan, was our house, its lights on, too, by now, and my mother, already setting the table.

Time to come in. Time for dinner. Play's over, the whistle meant at such times. But our call had its romantic connotations, too, though these concerned me only indirectly. It turned out that my father had used it as a signal to my mother in their courting days. He had had to, in fact, since it seemed that throughout most of their courtship her parents had disapproved of him—but here the real facts of the matter were obscured by that mixture of affectionate innuendo and nostalgic allusiveness that is always confusing to a child when he is listening to grownups. I was never quite sure what was true about the episode and what was a sort of intimate legendry. There was some exaggeration, certainly, for when my father maintained that at one point he had actually been forbidden the house, my mother denied it hotly.

"That's not true, Fred!" she cried. "You were always welcome."

"Not as welcome as Lennie Boyce," my father said dryly, and that confused me still further, for they had often spoken of Lennie Boyce as one of their oldest friends in New Haven, and now here he was suddenly being presented as a rival, and hence presumably as an enemy. Didn't grownups have any permanent feelings at all? "Oh, yes," my father went on. "They were high-class people indeed, the Davidsons." But now he had put on that extra solemnity that always made me suspect he was joking. "They couldn't abide me."

"And that's not true, either!" my mother retorted. "It wasn't you, and you know it. It was some of your friends they objected to."

At this, my father widened his eyes in what seemed to be utter astonishment. "*My* friends?" he demanded.

"You know what I mean," my mother said. It was then that I learned, to my surprise, that my father had been something of a blade in his younger days. In an amateur way, he had even gone in for boxing, then a thoroughly discredited sport. He had had a gym fitted out, with a regulation ring, in the carriage house back of his family's place, and he and some of his like-minded friends had worked out there diligently; they had even had a professional fighter as their trainer, and had backed him, in turn, in the ring.

"Growler Rourke," my father said reminiscently. "And a pretty good fighter, too, if he'd been willing to leave the bottle alone."

"Humph! Isn't that the trouble with all of them?" said my mother.

"I don't know about that. I wasn't so bad myself, dear."

"As if that was anything to boast of—fighting!" she retorted. For my own part, I was just staring at him, and not entirely approvingly, either. Kids at the age I was then are conservative; they don't want anything to disturb the pattern of their universe, and this sudden picture of my sedate father as a roisterer was definitely disconcerting.

"Well, anyway," my father said, and now he had turned to me. But I realized he was still talking to my mother, through me; I was a sounding board, so to speak, and this made me a trifle uncomfortable. "That's the reason I used to stand out on Dixwell Avenue and whistle—it was the only way I could get hold of her. She'd come to my whistle."

"Not to your whistle, sir!" my mother said. She had flushed, and this, as quite possibly she knew, was far from being to her disadvantage. My mother had that unusual combination, red hair and hazel eyes; she had a very white skin, as well, and the light flush made her look more attractive than ever. "I'd come to *you*," she added, and from the very tone of her voice I knew that everything was all right.

Our signal—or what shall I call it, our theme song, our motif?—saved me once, if not from serious trouble, at least from something close to it. That was when, playing on the dump of my father's mine out in Cripple Creek, or the Cripple Creek district, I wandered too close to the edge, slipped over, and then, for the life of me, couldn't get back. I was only about ten at the time, and my memory of the episode—even aided by what I was told about it later—is rather fragmentary. What I do recall of it, though, I remember vividly, for I was pretty well scared before it was over.

There is something grim and a little monstrous about a mine dump; anyway, it seems so to me. Inherently ugly—as ugly as its name, in fact—it is a kind of retching up of the shattered rock fetched forth from inside the earth, and however barren the region it lies in, it always looks out of place in the countryside.

In a way, too, it is a monument, inchoate but massive, to the drudgery of mining, for it, of course, is the repository only of the waste rock blasted and dug out in the worming search for the veins where the ore lies. The ore is shipped out elsewhere, to be ground down, milled, and refined. The dump begins where the shaft does, at the place of the first drilling down into the earth, and it grows and grows remorselessly as the shaft goes deeper and the sideward tunneling becomes more widespread—grows, indeed, until finally it dwarfs the hoist house and the other buildings that form the visible evidence of a mine's underground workings. And it remains as a tumbled testimony to the time, the effort, and the frustrations, undergone in the search for the gold itself.

Our mine was only one of many that were scattered below and around us, their dumps terracing the steeply slanting mountainside. But it was a fairly big one, for our holding was a subsidiary—called the "Lillie," I remember—of the big Vindicator Mine, and my father had merely leased it, as a venture. It was a "good producer," though, as they said out there. It had been worked before, and heavily; and the dump, in consequence, had grown large enough to have a rickety little railway, tramcar size, running out along the top of it, so that the rock sent up from below could be pushed out from the shaft head and dumped at the farther end.

All this—the size and the considerable extent of trackage —gave it an appearance of solidity. But this was illusory. The dump looked mountainous, but it lacked the coherence of a mountain. Like all those around and below it, it was the debris of a mountain. It was a mountain turned inside out, a pile of broken, uprooted rock set down loosely, and its slopes were held in place at their fixed angle not by roots and vegetation, but only by the most delicate balance between their tendency to obey the force of gravity and start rolling and their frictional resistance to it.

This is a condition that I have since learned is called by the pleasant phrase "the angle of repose," and almost anything—even the addition of so small a weight as mine was at the time—can disturb it. Though I didn't know the name or the facts of it, I discovered its practical implications on the day I'm speaking of, when I fell, or slipped, over the edge of our own dump. I landed only a few feet down, but even that was far enough, for when I tried to climb back up, I found that I couldn't make it. The very slidingness of the slope was against me. Whenever I moved, the mountain moved with me, but in the opposite direction; any toe hold or handhold I tried for in the loose rubble gave way instantly beneath me, and the more I tried to scramble up, the more surely I slid down.

Rather oddly, I didn't yell, or I don't recall that I did.

Even if I had, no one could have heard me back at the mine shaft, far out as I was on the dump. In my own recollection, though, something kept me quiet—stubbornness, perhaps; or maybe the fact that I wasn't supposed to be out there at all, and felt guilty, for ordinarily on my visits to the mine, I was supposed to stay close to the buildings around the shaft head.

The rest, for me, has a kind of nightmare quality. I had no way of knowing if or when a search for me started, and in fact it was quite a little time before one did. My father, luckily, was topside that afternoon. But he had other things to occupy him, running a mine, and it was a while before he missed me. All I knew was that I was in trouble, and the trouble was worsening.

There I was, clinging to that treacherous slope, and no matter what I did I got nowhere, or, rather, I got nowhere but down. I would claw and scramble for a while, but it was only to slide farther. I'd stay still for a while, but that wasn't satisfactory, either, for there was something threatening about the loom of that brownish-white, broken rock face before and around me; inevitably, I'd start scrambling again. I must have got a good halfway down it before I heard my father alternately calling my name and whistling. It is a sign of how deeply established our signal was that I whistled back.

"My God!" he cried—but in relief, not in anger or reproof—when, peering along the edge of the dump, he finally located me. "Just stay there. Don't move, don't do anything. Just *stay* there!" he told me. And I did, while he sent a man back to the hoist house for some rope and then slid down it. With the man above belaying and my father helping me, it was easy enough to climb back.

For a long while, I was of two minds about the amount

of danger I had been in at the time. On the face of it, it seems such a trivial affair—a mere false step or two and then a sliding—and I was surprised at my father's obvious relief when I was rescued. He told me later, though, that there were a number of things that had scared him.

As I have said, our mine was only one in the maze of shafts and dumps that formed the Vindicator and other workings. There was a whole series of them, falling like a frozen, rocky cascade down the mountainside below us. Worse still, scattered in among them, more or less at random, there were a number of older, abandoned mine shafts, some of them no more than a hole in the ground, but a fairly deep one; and they offered real danger to the unwary.

These were the "grubstake holes," some of them dating back to the district's beginnings, and they marked the site of some hopeful prospector's—or, more commonly, two such hopefuls': one to do the digging and blasting below and the other to tend the windlass—frustrated quest for fortune. The initial equipment required would hardly be more than would be needed to dig a well, at first, just a hand winch, some rope, a bucket, plus a hand drill, a sledge, a shovel, and some blasting powder; and if the money ran out or the site proved unpromising, it was easy enough to dismantle the whole setup and move it elsewhere.

The district abounded with these holes, some carelessly boarded over and some left open, and even veterans of the region walked warily over unknown ground, in consequence. The day, too, was drawing in, and I can realize now that my father had good reason to worry, for if I had got lost down below and night had fallen, I might have been in serious trouble. It was no doubt because of all this that he became, for him, unexpectedly conspiratorial.

"Let's not tell your mother about this, now, shall we?"

he warned me, when he had got me brushed off and on firm ground again. My mother, at that time, anyway, took a rather frosty, "Eastern" view of the turbulent West, particularly as it affected me, and I can understand now that a part of his concern was a feeling of guilt about the dangers he had let me get involved in. "You know, it would just upset her," he went on, a little weakly, "it would just upset her, and now there's no need for doing that."

I promised, and I was the more surprised when the first thing he did when we got home was to tell her all about it, making me out to be something of a hero, or at least a Spartan, into the bargain. "He didn't yell, or scream, or anything," he told her. "If you'd just seen him, hanging on there . . ."

"He shouldn't have been there in the first place," my mother replied. But she didn't say it sharply, and I gathered that she didn't mind, really; it occurred to me that maybe she was a little bit proud of me, too.

 **two**

One of the sharpest facets of my recollections of our Cripple Creek days is the thunderstorms we had out there. They came regularly, every day, throughout the summer, and with tremendous violence, and my memories of them are the clearer, perhaps, because one of them was the occasion of the first real quarrel that I can recall between my mother and my father.

I was around eight years old at the time (I was seven, I know, when we moved out there) and, as of course it would be bound to do to a boy from Connecticut set down suddenly in the midst of a real live mining camp, nearly everything about the place fascinated me: the rutted, rocky, board-sidewalked streets and the hammer of the men's booted feet on them as the mine's shifts changed; the mines fringing the town, their gaunt shaft houses or even gaunter gallows-frames squatting on the inevitable dumps of waste rock; the hills that rose all around us—Squaw Mountain, Battle Mountain, Bull Hill, and so on—green or tawny but always treeless, for, at altitudes ranging from eight thousand to more than ten thousand feet, the region was well above timber line; the spacious mountain air and the feeling of freedom it carried with it.

I know now that at the time I was there, around 1906, the camp's fortunes were already beginning to wane. The Cripple Creek regions had been something of an anomaly among mining camps in the first place. As geologists could tell you now, the gold-bearing area there—all confined within a rough circle about twenty miles in diameter—is in fact the filled-in crater of an ancient, extinct volcano, originally as huge, no doubt, as the craters on the moon; and the hills, now fairly rounded, that enclose it are merely the eroded remnants of the crater's once mighty ramparts, as the ridges and valleys that crisscross it are the result of the alternate eruptions and subsidences that occurred eons ago when the volcano was active.

All this implied that the structure of the rock inside the crater, far from being continuous, was in a kind of frozen turmoil, with sections of strata (and I'm speaking now of areas anywhere from a few hundred yards square to a mile or more) upended, laid crosswise, and turned every which way. However, the understanding of these facts was arrived at only fairly late in the camp's existence. Miners, it must be remembered, burrow in the dark, like moles, seeing only as far as the shaft's or the tunnel's end and then only dimly, by their candles' or their lamps' light; and the geological crazy quilt they were confronted with at Cripple Creek was for a long time completely baffling.

Gold was found in lodes, or pockets, and some of these were of incredible richness. (One such, an underground cavern or hollow in the rock, called a geode, at the Cresson Mine, some forty feet high and around twenty feet square, and literally lined with gold, yielded close to $1,200,000.) But the lode, inexplicably, might be completely isolated, in the midst of barren territory. Gold was found in veins, but the veins, rich and promising, might snuff out suddenly against a wall of alien rock. Gold was found near the surface and it was found at depth. One result of this topsy-turviness was that although the area was a nightmare to the conventionally trained metallurgist, it was a paradise for the tyro.

In fact, to the trained man, his background of experience was a handicap, for his very training tended to mislead him. Gold, in the Cripple Creek district, was literally where you found it; the whole thing was catch-as-catch-can, and the lore of the place was full of stories, later relayed to me, of the part sheer luck had played in the fortunes that had been made there in the early days.

There was the mine called The Pharmacist, near the top of Bull Hill, overlooking Victor—an unlikely spot, it seemed, but the mine turned out to be exceptionally profitable. It was founded by a couple of drugstore clerks, up for a visit from Denver to see what all the excitement was about, who decided that, being there, they might as well take a fling at the thing. It was literally a fling, too, for they were sitting on the top of the hill at the time, and in a spirit of ebullience one of them, a soon-to-be millionaire named Arthur D. Jones, scaled his hat down the hillside, and started digging where it fell. The Pharmacist yielded well over five million dollars within a decade, and I only wish that some anterior relative of mine, an uncle or a great-uncle, had had sense enough to be in the area at the time of the bonanza. So much depends on the wisdom, the practicality, and the faculty of just *being there* on the part of one's antecedents.

There was the Gold Coin, which started as a hotel to be erected on the town of Victor's main street and was transformed abruptly into a mine when the blasting for the basement disclosed a twenty-inch-thick vein. There was the Portland, which I spoke of earlier, located by a three-dollar-a-day carpenter from Colorado Springs named Winfield Scott Stratton, and which in less than six months' time from the staking of the claim had made him Cripple Creek's first millionaire. I used to wonder why my father had not had sense enough to get out to the region, say, ten years sooner than he did.

A half-share of the Elkton Mine, a grubstake operation to begin with, was made over to a Cripple Creek grocery man, to pay off a $36.50 food bill, and the grocer probably made the deal reluctantly; in those early days everyone was trying to foist off mine shares instead of cash on the local merchants. The Elkton, when I last heard about it, had produced more than sixteen million dollars and was still in active operation. So tightrope-thin and so precarious, I learned then, is the edge between the lucky strike and disaster, for in listing the resounding successes, one tends to forget the failures, and, still more, the workaday mines, like my father's, that just paid their way.

There is one sad, inescapable fact about any mining area: It is a repository only, and so, in the end, exhaustible. By the time we got there, less than twenty years after gold had first been found in the region, the real boom was over. No new strikes were being made, for the whole area had been pretty well explored. Most of the existing mines were gradually being bought up by outside interests and either merged or leased out piecemeal to individual adventurers. The wilder days were over and the era of businesslike practicality was setting in.

The truth is that, apart from Altman, Independence, and a few other small, rip-roaring settlements that were scattered about among the hills, the Cripple Creek district had always been what was known as a "family camp"—as distinguished from the really tough, hell-raising towns like Leadville, where the males roamed loose and the only feminine influence to be found was in the cribs and the dance halls.

But it was wild enough for me, and when a group of cowboys rode in, jingle jangle, from some one of the ranches that still operated in the valleys round about; or a man walked past with the bulge of his gun showing plainly beneath the sober black coat he was wearing; or when shots rang out somewhere off in the town, late at night, and I heard them as I lay bedded in my room, I watched or listened in both awe and fascination.

But there was something disturbing about all this, too, and the thunderstorms were part of this general feeling. We had settled first in Victor, which was, next to Cripple Creek itself, the largest town in the district. But transportation in that mountainous region was difficult. The mines lay scattered everywhere. And since my father's little mine, the Lillie, lay some distance off in the hills, in the Elkton area, we moved nearer and nearer to it, as opportunity offered—to, eventually, the tiny settlement of Christmas Crossing, where we were practically on top of the workings.

The trouble was that my mother, at the start at least, just did not like being in the West at all, and this moving about only added to her confusion. (Later on, of course, as she made a few friends and accustomed herself to the strange new atmosphere, she settled into things cheerfully; later still, when we had come back east, she was often heard to boast, a bit romantically, about the hardships and the perils we'd encountered there.) I can see now, though, that in the beginning she was as intimidated as I was, and even more apprehensive.

A New Englander, and in many ways a true Victorian (though she was also a woman of considerable spirit), she regarded the whole life of the place as rough, untutored, and menacing; and although it would have been picturesque enough on a visit (as had been our first intention), when she learned that my father had been tempted to try mining himself for a while, her attitude stiffened. When she found herself actually immersed in it—when my father would go off with his lunch pail and candle clip, a pair of overalls rolled under his arm like any other miner, and come home gray with dust and dried muck, for, to anyone connected with it, from owner on down, mining is likely to be a messy business—her reaction must have been desperate indeed.

So I realize now that there was a certain amount of dissension between my parents all through that Cripple Creek period—not serious or ineradicable, for they were a deeply loving couple, but, as long as the conditions that caused it existed, constant. I can see now, too, that my mother was mostly worried about me.

She was determined that I, at least, should not be contaminated, and so, through the early part of our stay there, she did her best to make me a little island of Eastern propriety in that vast roily sea of Western freedom. I wore knee pants and long stockings, as a proper boy should, while the other boys generally wore overalls. I was kept close to home, for the most part, and not allowed to run about too much, or wander, for my mother was afraid that the altitude might in some way affect me; and once I was out of her sight, her mind was instantly filled with thoughts of all the other dread things that might be happening to me.

All this, though, was a part of her early reaction, and she

modified it later, for the district was not only a "family" camp; it was also a friendly place and in many ways a curiously sophisticated one. People who think of gold camps solely as assemblages of whorehouses, barrooms, and shanties are thinking in movie terms. To be sure, the barrooms and whorehouses were there, and apparently heavily patronized. They were in plain sight, too, for in Victor, as in most other mining towns, for some reason, the red-light district lay just by the railroad station, and whenever we went anywhere by rail, which was fairly often in that pre-automobile era, we had to walk through it. In its way, it was probably a salutary experience for Victorian ladies like my mother. For my own part, I often wondered—I'm afraid at times audibly—why *we* didn't have a basket of flowers or a bouquet painted on the door, and our name surrounded by curlicues. My mother, at such times, paid no heed and just hurried me on.

People, though, who think in such terms forget the enormous attraction gold has, and how far-reaching its influence is; most magnetic of metals, it will attract men from everywhere. And if Cripple Creek, as I've said, was even then past its peak, no one, except possibly the shrewdest operators, knew it. It was, in fact, world famous, and as a result people came from all over the world—some from curiosity, more to make the gamble—to sample its excitements.

This gave it, as well as other towns, a cosmopolitan flavor that is rarely mentioned in accounts of the old gold camps. Welsh and Cornish men came to swell the ranks of the working miners. British younger sons and young men fresh from the Eastern colleges—young married men, too, like my father—came out for a year or two to try their luck before settling down to a job in their fathers' businesses or something equally prosaic. And the easy prosperity of the place drew in others. Musicians, lecturers, and famous actors and actresses on tour with their troupes made it a port of call, and some of the less well-known ones stayed, to add to the glamour of the place. I remember an Italian ballet dancer—lean, graceful, and whiplike, with a gaunt, pale, beautiful face—who abandoned the troupe she was with and remained to give dancing lessons, and, probably, dabble in mining stocks. There was a large, sad Russian, a former jeweler in Saint Petersburg, who functioned part time as an assayer, and made incredibly delicate jewelry on the side. And I think one of the high points of my mother's career out there was a tea she gave for Eugene Ysaye, the Belgian violinist (about all I recall of him is a small, sharp-chinned gnomish face underneath a tremendous shock of very white hair—but then, I was allowed only to peek in at the party) at which he actually played! A recital by a world-famous violinist, right in our own living room— that, she had to admit, was something that could never have happened to people like us back east!

That was later, though, for at the start fears rode her constantly—not only for my father, deep down in the close darkness of the mine workings, but for all three of us—and these were such a mixture of the just and wildly exaggerated that they laid her open continually to my father's teasing and yet, occasionally, provided her with the meager satisfactions (and the frustrations) of a Cassandra. After all, boys—and men, too—now and then did fall into abandoned mine shafts, and in the mines themselves men were caught by explosions or overwhelmed by the fall of rock; hunters roaming in the hills were attacked by wolves or mountain lions.

My father laughed, but she, and I, quivered, and I realize

now that, quite unwittingly, she was in a fair way to ruining my whole life there if the storms, and my father—and, eventually, her own good sense—hadn't intervened.

I was lonely. My Eastern clothes and, I suppose, my general air of being a "mama's boy" set me apart from the other kids, and made me feel out of place there. I kept all this to myself, of course; since my parents did not confide in me, so—and so it is always between generations—I could not confide in them. Certainly, till the quarrel, I had no idea that either of them was concerned about me, or that there was any difference between them.

I just got along by myself, pretty much of the time. I read a great deal, puzzling my way through books that were actually far beyond my age (I imagine I'm one of the very few people alive who read Bulwer Lytton's *Last Days of Pompeii* at the age of nine—all the way through, too, and of course, understanding almost nothing of it), and if some of this was done because I hadn't much else to do, I didn't tell anyone. Like my mother, I was frightened a little by the strangeness; of all the many places I lived in as a child, Victor is the only one where I can't recall the name of a single friend or companion.

The thunderstorms, as I've said, were part of this general feeling; and these were slashing, flashing affairs of a kind of uproarious violence that I have never seen equalled elsewhere, and that somehow seemed to fit the very spirit of the district itself. We encountered them first in Victor, and from then on it was a rare day, all through that first spring and summer, when we didn't have one. They came, too, with a queer sort of punctuality.

Around four o'clock every afternoon, the sky would darken. Clouds—clouds that had seemed harmless before; big, fat, cottony sunset clouds merely lingering behind the peaks—would grow, gather, tower, and then rush down upon us. There would have been rumblings before, of course, and the kind of shuddering, light-flashings that occur on the periphery of the heavens. But the storms came so suddenly that these were no real warning or preparation. The clouds, the darkness, the lightning came and overwhelmed us with an appalling swiftness—and then what fury would be unloosed!

Rain would come first, torrentially, and then hail, and the hail would rip down with such savage violence that horses, especially, were driven wild by it. It was the accepted custom for their riders or drivers to shelter them anywhere, and I can still recall seeing ore teams driven up under the wooden awnings commonly built over the plank sidewalks in Victor, the horses stamping and stumbling on the unfamiliar footing and the drivers standing at their heads, holding them tight-bitted, people skirting them cautiously, till the storm had passed.

Meantime, there were the thunder, the lightning—thunder loud enough to stun the ears, and the lightning great, flaring bolts whose very breadth and brilliance showed the closeness of their origin—and the sheeted, cascading downpour.

Afterward, the sun shining again, the air crisp and almost acid with ozone, the whole world looking washed and glittering, I would be allowed to go out and sail wood chips, solemnly, on the brown rush of water that now filled the deep gullies on either side of the street.

The storms, fortunately, were as brief as they were violent, but to my mother they were one more menace to be lived through, a sort of polarization of the dangers that threatened us. My father, contrarily, delighted in them, and so the storms became one more of the dividing points that

separated my mother and father all through that period. I
think I sensed this, vaguely, but I was some time in realizing
that I was also involved in the situation. We were at Christmas Crossing by then, and the storms had followed us; in
a sense, it was almost as if we had climbed up farther into
them.

The Crossing, though it lay actually on a saddle between
two higher peaks, was, at close to eleven thousand feet of
altitude, a sort of eminence of its own. East and west, we
could look out almost illimitably—in the early mornings,
over a sea of white vaporous clouds that still held the valleys blanketed while we stood in bright sunshine; through
the day, at the tumble of lesser hills and valleys, dotted here
and there with towns and settlements, clogged with mines
and these all noisy with the sound of pumps, hoists, and
compressors, their steep-roofed red- or black-painted
buildings always dust-coated—on a view that went on un-
hindered to the peaks of the Sangre de Cristos, a good
seventy miles south and west of us; and by night, at the
twinkling clusters of lights from the towns and the isolated
ones from the solitary cabins, and at the hot smoky glare
from the mine buildings below.

We were literally among the clouds there. When the
storms came, we were among them, too; we were even inside them, and when one was at its height, we had not only
the tumult without, but in the house itself, frequently, static
flowed, rippling in little livid green-and-blue streams along
the wiring and the electric fixtures, and exploding sometimes in midair, erratically, in tiny, sharp, crackling sparks
that echoed, in miniature, the great bursts of thunder and
lightning outside.

To my mother, this must have been pretty much the last
straw. My father, naturally, had tried to prove to her that

the static was harmless, as already he had brought to bear all the usual arguments to convince her that the bark of the storm, so to speak, was far worse than its bite.

"If you hear the thunder," he'd say, "if you even see the lightning, you're safe."

But she'd shake her head stubbornly. "I don't *want* to see it," she would say.

He would stare at her silently, put off for the moment by her lack of logic, and a little exasperated. And when another storm came, having first shut the doors and shut the windows, she would retreat to her bedroom, where, the shades drawn, a towel, often, over her eyes, she would lie immobile on the bed until the storm had passed.

Like as not, I'd be in there with her, not so much either to protect her or to be protected, as just simply to *be* there with her, sharing, at whatever distance and dimness of comprehension, whatever it was that went on inside her. My father, by that time, if he were at home, would be out on the porch enjoying it, for he loved the storms, truly, as much as she feared them.

It seemed, indeed, almost as if he were drawn to them; after standing indoors for a while at one window or another to mark the flashes, and then moving to the doorway to see them better ("Fred! Fred! Shut that door!" my mother would be calling from her refuge in the bedroom. "Do you want to kill us all?"), he would wind up inevitably on the porch, in his own kind of freedom. I can still see him there, stamping back and forth as the storm veered, soaked with rain, perhaps, as the gusts whipped in, but oblivious—yelling in to us, more or less unintelligibly, in sheer exultation at the might and the excitement of it. (I would have tiptoed to the door by then, and closed it.)

So, again, there was division between them, and I hovered

uncertainly in the midst of it. But then, how can a man describe the problems and trials of his childhood? It seems to me that a child lives on the lower levels of a tall, tiered series of adult experiences, and I remember once, with my father, in the drafting room of the Vindicator, being shown what I even then realized was the master survey of the whole mine's workings.

It is one of those odd, isolated recollections with which everyone's remembrance is studded, and it fascinated me, for the survey had been made by "levels," duplicating the tiers of tunnels which, like the floors of a building, took off horizontally from the descending shaft. Since the drawings had been done on the waxed, almost transparent sheets that draftsmen call "tracing cloth," and they were now kept racked one above the other in a cabinet built specially for them, the result was that one could pull out the survey on any one level and have, at a glance, a map of its workings or, conversely—and it was this that fascinated me—look down through the whole lot of them and see, clearly at the top and then more dimly, where one tunnel crossed another below it and was crossed, in its turn, by the tunnel above.

So, it seems to me, it is when one looks back at one's childhood—through a veining upon veining of purposes and cross-purposes, up through which, too, the child must struggle to reach manhood and comprehension.

All I know now, really, is that when the quarrel came, it came suddenly, as suddenly as the storms and as dramatically, and since in the midst of it my father did a violent thing, and he was a man slow to anger, I can only conclude that it must have been a climax of other quarrels, or differences at least, which had gradually built up to this one.

I know that one day, in the midst of a storm, my father came in, grabbed me by the hand, and led me out into it;

beyond that, the rest is fragmentary, and my next recollection is of all three of us indoors again, and my parents facing each other in anger. But I can still see them, both suddenly huge and strange as they reared above me, split apart and yet held, face to face, by their fury; shouting, too, while the storm roared and I crouched and quivered—snatched at, maybe, and then snatched back again, though I can't recall that—between them.

I can't recall the voices or what they were saying, though I can imagine them. ("You've gone crazy with this Western stuff, Fred! You'll kill him!" And my father: "By God, Hattie! You're ruining the boy!") And it surely must have been a culmination, for, abruptly, my father turned and, in one of those blind acts of meaningless violence that are no more than a venting, physically, of the torments of anger, seized a bedside table that stood near to his hand and slammed it down on the floor again, hard, so hard, indeed, for my father was strong, that he smashed it.

I can still see it lying there, splintered, and the things that had been upon it (a book, maybe, an alarm clock? I can't recall) tumbling on the floor.

I can't recall the voices, but I can imagine them, and, as I say, it must have been a culmination, for after it many things, things affecting my own life, changed abruptly, in that magical way they sometimes do for a child. Though my mother still worried needlessly over me, I was at last allowed to dress decently in overalls, and play duck-on-the-rock with the other boys, and a wild game of fox-and-geese (greatly expanded, in the Western fashion) that took us sometimes for miles and miles up and into the hills. I was even allowed to go down into my father's mine.

But all I know is that, suddenly, I was out on the porch with my father, and for a moment or so, in the blast of the storm, all I could do there was to stand against the wall by the door and cower.

I have an impression of my father coming at me, and I think now that for an instant he was going to slap me. But if so, he controlled himself; instead, he took me up in his arms. He was soothing me. "Look now, fellow," he was saying, or something like it; if I can't recall the words, I can recall the change in his mood. "It's not so bad now, really, is it? Look at *that* flash now, *those* flashes! Aren't they wonderful? Aren't they glorious?"

And suddenly, wonderfully, they were. It was at Christmas Crossing that this happened, and I watched many storms from that porch with my father afterward; afterward, indeed, we won my mother out to watch some of them, too. So it is the storms in the aggregate, so to speak, that I remember, instead of this or any other single one: the great rush and roar of them, and the feeling of being enveloped by a force so majestic, mighty, and impersonal that even its menace became an exhilaration, while the fact that one was able to stand up to it in its full power was both a challenge and a reward.

It was a good place to be with one's father and mother, united—most of all when, at last, the storm would be rolling out past us ("showing its heels to us," as my father put it), its lightnings still stab, stab, stabbing as fiercely as ever but now in the regions beyond and below; and one could feel its tensions relaxing in the air around us, as they had already relaxed in the house itself.

 three

Things narrow down as the years go on; the infinite prospects, the endless variety of possible outcomes that confront one, or seem to, when one is young tend to diminish inexorably as one grows older. The walls close in, and the exit, as one approaches it, gets not larger but smaller. I still remember, for instance, the moment when I decided (learned, rather; the fact was borne in on me) that I would never be really rich.

It was one of those clear, crisp days in early spring that have now become almost legendary, in our smog-smitten New York, when the very air seems to have a sparkle of its own, as the sun has its own special brilliance, spreading coolness and clarity, rather than warmth, over everything —and I was walking down Fifth Avenue. I was passing a row of shops somewhere below Fifty-seventh Street when a car pulled in to the curb just ahead of me.

It was a town car, black, sleek, polished, luxurious, and it had hardly stopped before a footman hopped out and opened the door, and a woman—a very pretty woman, too, slim, hatless, with an oval face, white-skinned, and hair as sleekly black as the car itself—stepped to the pavement.

She was furred, and she wore the furs carelessly; she was jeweled, she was exquisite. She was also abstracted, or else so completely assured that she felt no need to defer to others, for she gave not a glance to any of us who were passing at the time; we made way for her as she walked quickly across the sidewalk and into one of the shops.

I never saw her again, that I know of. But I remember the whole thing vividly, for it was then, on seeing her, that I was seized with a sudden realization of the amount of sheer wealth there must be—*had* to be—in the background, to produce this swift, lovely apparition.

In a way, the moment had the quality of a real revelation, for I remember thinking, too, of the thousands of tiny details, each one costly and necessary, and, above all, long-accustomed, that were implicit in the episode, from the car that was not only washed but dusted daily (and the carriage house, still maintained on some side street uptown, and the men—the chauffeur, the footman—who did the washing and dusting) to the maids, the laundress, the cook, and all the rest of the household who clothed, fed, pampered, and cared for this precious creature; in short, the wealth (and, I felt sure, the long-accumulated, established wealth) that was involved in and was essential to every moment of her existence.

As I say, I never saw the lady again, and indeed I had no desire to. She was in her middle thirties, for one thing, which made her an "older woman" in my eyes. I don't want, either, to make it seem that I felt in any way mournful or even wistful about the episode. As a matter of fact, I was not only impressed, I was also appalled by the complications that wealth, as I suddenly realized, carried with it; being rich, for a bohemian like myself, might very possibly be the least bit boring.

Or being *that* rich, anyway. I can't tell precisely why that revelation should have come over me at that particular moment on Fifth Avenue; in fact, at first glance it seems odd that it should have happened so, for I had just come back from a stay of some years in France, and I had seen there, many times, handsomer and more exotic cars— Isottas, Hispanos, Bugattis—with even more glamorous women riding in them. Yet it occurs to me now, mightn't that have been part of the reason? The wealth I'd seen abroad was French wealth, and so a little unreal and mysterious, as the women I saw descending from theirs cars in front of the shops along the rue de la Paix were French, too, and hence equally remote and mysterious.

That day, though, I was on my own home grounds. The money here was reckoned in millions, not in milliards, and it was not in francs but in dollars—the kind that I had in my pockets, except that I had fewer of them. And—I don't know—there may have been other impulses involved that I don't remember now.

All this happened in the early nineteen-twenties, when I was in my early twenties myself. I was a writer, or I wanted to be one, and though I knew that the occupation was generally considered to be unremunerative, I didn't want to work at anything else any more than I had to.

So I dreamed, instead, of some undemanding but still life-sustaining job (as a railroad-crossing tender, maybe, where I could write away cozily in my little shack between trains) or, alternatively, of some sudden coup (a stock-market tip, say, that I played astutely, pyramiding a small initial investment right up into thousands, then tens and even hundreds of thousands) that would relieve me forever of any financial worries.

And till then—and, till then, it had been my family that

had largely supported me—it had been dreams like this that had buffered me against reality. I suppose it was the sense of reality that caught up with me that day on Fifth Avenue. At any rate, I can still recall the definiteness and the clarity—the quietness of it, too, for my mood was not envious or resentful; one doesn't quarrel with finality—of the thought that crossed my mind as the woman crossed the sidewalk before me: I shall never, really, be rich.

I can't recall now, precisely, the moment when I knew my parents weren't rich, weren't just as rich and as powerful as anyone else in the world. At the outset of a child's life, his parents *are* the world. They are everything, the all-wise, the all-deciding; they are his omnipotent omnipresent shield, and it is only later, and by degrees—and in some cases, I imagine, painfully—that he learns they are not supreme in everything, that there are other people who are stronger, wiser, more capable than they.

I was lucky in that respect. In the first place, because my father was a true man of impulse, and given to wandering. (I once figured out that I went to eight different grammar and high schools, altogether, before I got away to college, and to a comparatively sedentary life of my own, but I may have left out a couple along the way.) In the second place, when my father did settle down—if that's the proper word for it—it was to a violently variable career. What he would do, in other words, was pile up a sort of grubstake by working as a designer of special machinery and then devote it to developing one of his never-quite-perfected inventions (which, of course, when completed, was going to make us millions), and our economic life, in consequence, was subject to such wild ups and downs that not only I but my parents themselves scarcely knew where we were at from one day to another.

There were, of course, the revelatory moments when—
Well, why can't I have a bicycle? All the other kids have
one! And why are we having rice pudding so much, all of
a sudden, instead of chocolate layer cake? There were the
times, too, when the atmosphere grew vaguely disquieting,
when I'd hear my parents talking, not freely and cheerfully, but soberly and low, mysteriously, long after my
bedtime.

But for the most part, mistakenly or not, they tried to
keep their money troubles from me, and as far as I can recall,
it wasn't until I was about fifteen that I really came up
against the facts of our life, financially, and then it was in
such a mixture of the dramatic, the ludicrous, and the
purely loving that the incident was robbed of any un-
pleasantness.

We had come east by that time. We were living in New
York, and it occurs to me now that my father, coming east,
may have found himself faced with something like the same
shift in values that I encountered coming back to New
York from Paris, for in a sense, in the West, when we were
there, the atmosphere was bohemian, too. In the mining
regions, money, of itself, was inconsequential—or, say,
rather, it existed in that most rarefied area of all, the future.

As in Montparnasse, where every man was a genius until
he had written his book or painted his picture, so, out there,
any man who had a mine—a hole in the ground, or the
start of one—was, potentially, the equal of the Strattons,
the Penroses, or any other of the already almost mythical
figures who had made their fortunes in the district. Gold
was there; all a man had to do was to find it, as these men
had done, and that might happen to anyone, one day. And,
as a matter of fact, my father had not done badly in his
mining venture, for a green Easterner.

He had made no great "strikes," to be sure; as I've already said, the day of the really big strike was over in the district. But he had leased a couple of claims, and had worked them capably, emerging with enough to finance a leisurely trip farther out, to the Coast, and still have something left over for the start in the East; and I can see now that it may well have been quite a change for both my father and my mother to come from that hopeful, euphoric atmosphere to the hard-and-fast, matter-of-fact one of New York.

We had been in one of our up periods, in other words, and now we were going through one of our downs. But I didn't realize this, or even begin to, until I called for my father late one December afternoon, to do our Christmas shopping. I called for him after school, at a little machine shop he had set up, downtown, for his experiments, and the scene itself, as it comes back to my mind, has a certain Dickensian flavor: the slush, and the wintry streets and sidewalks, dark except where the light from shop windows struck across them; the rush and the noise of the traffic; and the excitement, over and under it all, of the approaching holidays.

It was only my father's mood that seemed out of keeping. My father was an old-line Yankee by birth, but in most ways he was the antithesis of the traditional Yankee type. He was plump and cheerful rather than lanky and taciturn, generous instead of penny-pinching. But here we were, starting out on what should have been a lively expedition and yet he stalked along glum and largely silent beside me.

When he talked, it was mainly about economy. "We've really got to go easy on everything this year. Your mother says so herself, and she's right," he said once. We were heading toward Wanamaker's—I guess because it was my mother's favorite store—and we had stopped in front of a women's-wear shop to look at a display of stockings. Stockings, at least, would be practical.

"Things aren't going as fast as I'd like them to at the shop," he went on as we started off again. (Stockings, it appeared, were a little *too* practical.) "Not that it's anything for you to worry about, boy. We'll make out all right; we always have.

"And this time I really think I'm on the edge of something. Something big," he added, as we paused again, in front of a household-supplies store, its windows full of casseroles, coffeepots, double boilers, and so on.

"No, no. She does enough cooking," he said restlessly, and we moved on once more. So it went, until we got to Wanamaker's.

I still remember the brilliance and animation of the place, with its profusion of lights and decorations all centering on the big rotunda as we came in.

Department stores were really palaces of commerce then, or they seemed so to a boy fresh from the West. I had little time to enjoy the spectacle, though. Wanamaker's had a *boutique*, in those days, called "Coin de Paris" and set apart fastidiously in a corner of the main floor. It featured especially choice pieces of jewelry, among other things, and we stopped there. And within minutes, it seemed, my father had bought an antique necklace of the kind called a "lavaliere"—a fine silver chain strung with amethyst pendants.

I don't remember the price, though it was obviously high. And I didn't realize the enormity of what my father had done until Christmas morning, when my mother opened the package it came in, looked at the necklace a moment and then at my father, and then, to my utter bewilderment, burst into tears.

"Fred! Fred! How could you!" she cried.

To my still greater horror, my father jumped up and began yelling at her. Suddenly, all was pandemonium—my mother in tears and my father stamping about, red-faced and angry-looking—and, as far as I could see, for no reason.

"I won't wear it! I won't even touch it! You'll have to take it back!" she was crying.

And he was shouting, "God damn it, Hattie! Will you listen to me? Will you listen? We looked all over town for something cheap!"

"Cheap!" she cried. My mother was Scotch-Irish, and easily as emotional as he. But she was cannier about money, or perhaps she'd just had to become so, as a counter to his impulsiveness, and so she had been cast as the balance wheel, financially, of the family. This time, though, as he did almost always, he overrode her.

"Yes, *cheap!*" he cried, louder than she. "But I just couldn't do it. Damn it, you deserve this!"

"Deserve it?" she said, and, again inexplicably, she burst out laughing. Watching, I knew everything was going to be all right.

We were living on Edgecombe Avenue, then, on the heights above Morningside Park and, beyond that, the upper reaches of Harlem. It was a dreary region. We had just dropped there, somehow, coming from the West; even then, we weren't that poor. And it was the drearier for me because the school I had been sent to was way downtown and I had no contacts, scholastic or otherwise, with the other kids in the neighborhood. Our Christmas, before the necklace appeared, had been a careful, conservative, economical one.

In a way, though—a way that my father surely could not have foreseen—the necklace made the day. To my father, I suppose, it was a promise, as to my mother it was intended as reassurance, and in the end she accepted it in that fashion.

Suddenly, everything was gay. We forgot the dismal little flat and the run-down neighborhood, and when my mother sat down to dinner, in her best dress and with the necklace gleaming at her throat, I remember thinking that she had never looked prettier. Once, she put her hand up and touched it.

"But the bills, Fred!" she protested. As many women will, she couldn't help mixing her pleasure with practicality; in a sense, it was a way of propitiating the future. "And the end of the month so near! How'll we ever pay them? You know I'll never be able to wear this with a clear conscience till those bills are paid."

"We'll pay them," my father said stoutly, and I'm sure we did. Indeed, I think the necklace may have been a turning point—of confidence, say, and encouragement—for soon after that, on my birthday, I *got* a bicycle, and soon after that we moved to Rochester and got a car. And if my mother's sole concern about the necklace was the bills, that must have righted itself, too, for it was still among her effects when she died.

 four

As anyone who has read this far must realize, the present book is a long way from being an autobiography in the formal sense, and this is not because I'm not old enough, either; I am. There are times, and they occur so often nowadays in New York, when I pass a building under demolition and see a sign announcing a new office building, fifty, sixty, seventy stories high and completely air-conditioned, to be ready for occupancy in 1970—or, again, when I recall Bertrand Russell's briskly boding prophecy that man will in all probability have succeeded in exterminating himself well before the end of this century—that I wonder, not wholly wistfully, yet not wholly gladly, either, if I will still be around at the time the building is opened, or, conversely, when it is in ruins.

No, I'm old enough, all right, at least in the matter of years; the truth lies in a different direction. The truth is that I haven't reached the point, philosophically, for the long, the considered view, the real summing-up. It would be presumptuous, for one thing, for I haven't done enough yet to warrant a work of that description; more than that, there are so many books, stories I want to write, so many things I want to do—and hope, too, to do—that it seems pointless now to sit back and, laboriously, draw up a balance sheet that I hope is still far from being the final accounting.

So this, then, is a book of casual reminiscence, random and episodic—random in the sense that I have made no attempt at chronological sequence, and episodic in that it is based, throughout, on happenings or observations that, slight as they sometimes were, had a certain significance which, in one way or another, made them memorable to me.

For all its formlessness, though, I imagine a brief bit of vital statistics is in order, if only as background.

I was born April 6, 1897, in New Haven, Connecticut; went to a number of schools (as I have stated), ranging from New Haven to Colorado and then back, via northern New York State and Massachusetts, ending up, again at New Haven, at college. I had, long before that, decided I wanted to be a writer—indeed, I find it hard to recall a time when I *didn't* want to be a writer—but since my first choice was poetry, and that clearly was not self-supporting, I had jobs. I worked briefly for a small, short-lived newspaper-feature agency (whose head, a large, charming, easygoing man named E. A. Moree, later sensibly dropped the whole business and became a bridge expert instead); quit that because Moree, one summer, wouldn't let me have my vacation at the same time as the girl I was going around with was having hers; worked then for the United States Rubber Company, writing "inspirational" pamphlets; and then, obeying some complex of impulses that is still a little obscure to me, made my way abroad, to France mostly—and by that gesture, I think, *became* a writer.

I have since learned that, by this act, I automatically became an "exile" and a part of the "Lost Generation." But

I didn't know this at the time. All I knew was that a girl I was fond of (a different girl, by the way: a painter) was already in Paris, and I wanted to be with her; some other friends were going, though as many more were not; I had some money saved, and my parents were willing to help with a grubstake. As I say, there was a complex of influences. But I still think the desire to get away from the full-time job, relegating writing to a hole-in-the-corner operation; the desire to live as a writer, to really *be* one, was paramount. But I want to leave the part about writing till later.

Though I've begun this book at random and intend to keep on so, I think it is impossible for anyone to contemplate his past for any length of time and at all intensively without finding himself involved in a certain amount of metaphysical speculation. Concepts, even of oneself, seem to scatter a little. One looks back and sees the youngster there, the boy *there*, then the youth, the man. Or, searching for dates and reminders, one comes upon ancient photographs, letters, writings, and other memorabilia long thought lost. Meanwhile, aided by these, the mind re-creates the faraway, changing background; stimulated still further, the senses, with their chancy, mysterious mixture of forgetfulness and retentiveness, bring back vividly and in all their freshness and immediacy, a sound, a smell, a remembrance of the way the air felt or the sunlight fell at a given moment, to enliven the long-gone atmosphere.

And the problem is how to sort these entities out, find a system or progression in the development of all these changing, variable I's, each one shaping and at the same time altering the next—above all, how to cram them into the I, aging, vulnerable, seemingly fixed but still, no doubt, itself alterable and imperceptibly altering, that exists today.

There are so many strings leading back into the past. Let me give an example. The other day, I was pacing back and forth alone in the living room of my apartment when, for no particular reason that I can think of—except that I was stuck in the middle of a story and at such times am likely to be both restless and abstracted—I found myself walking in a peculiar fashion. Its characteristic was that I was putting my toe down at each step *before* the heel, in a way that I believe is generally called "Indian fashion" for, supposedly, it is the way they were able to move so silently along their forest paths. To me, though, it has another connotation, and as soon as I realized what I was doing, I knew who I was, where I was, and what period I had reverted to in my past.

Some others who were growing up at the same time may already have recognized my identity. To them, it will be apparent immediately that I was Jack London's Wolf Larsen, pacing the rolling deck of his schooner the *Sea Wolf*, with that catlike, distinctive tread that enabled him to turn up, disconcertingly, at the very elbows of the hero and heroine, his captives aboard the vessel, at the very moment they were plotting how to disable him and make their getaway.

I was back, in short, in my youth again. It was not, even then, that I liked Wolf Larsen particularly. To mince no words about it, he was a conscienceless scoundrel, rough, rugged, and ruthless, and he played with his unwilling hostages in a manner as feline as his tread, terrorizing them as thoroughly as he did his fellow traders and pretty much everyone else in the South Seas. (Humphrey Van Weyden, the hero of the book, had been shanghaied inadvertently when he fell off a ferry in San Francisco harbor, and the heroine, Maud Brewster, had been hauled aboard after a shipwreck, farther out to sea, and any decent ship's captain would have set them both ashore at the nearest port. Did Wolf Larsen, though? Not he! He preferred to keep them on tenterhooks and see them suffer.)

But for all his rascality, he had a certain recklessness that I envied even as I deplored it, and, compared with the rather bookish hero, he was masculinity personified. (I was maybe fourteen at the time and looking forward, a bit apprehensively, to the privileges and obligations of manhood. I welcomed anything that seemed to offer guidance.) Mainly, though, it was that tread of his that fascinated me, and when afoot, at least, I was Wolf Larsen for quite a while during that stage of my development. It must have puzzled my parents considerably to have me sneaking around the house, toe and heel, toe and heel, and oh so silently, instead of clattering carelessly about as I'd always done until then.

But then, as I have had occasion to learn myself by now, parents have to get used to such sudden, mysterious changes in their offspring, though mine must have been more than ordinarily bemused, at another stage of things that occurred when I was around fifteen, to find me suddenly transformed from a kid who had to be heaved and harried out of bed mornings, in order to get him to school on time, into one who voluntarily was setting his alarm clock for six, and getting out in the chill, dim dawn to run about the neighboring streets in shorts and a T shirt for a half-hour or so before coming in for breakfast. I was being a distance runner then, a famous miler (whose name I have now forgotten) at Yale, who, I'd read somewhere, had made himself over from a puny youth to a champion by just such a process.

I was Bertrand DuGuesclin, too, for a while, the great

fourteenth-century soldier and Grand Constable of France, and his name still holds the very sound of the Middle Ages for me. I first ran across him in an early novel by Conan Doyle called *The White Company*. It is not one of his better-known works, nor is it even, I'm afraid, a very important one. But it held a peculiar fascination for me. I was about ten at the time, and it was almost as if it held a secret in its pages, tantalizing and endlessly elusive (about life? history? writing itself?). And as I suppose happens with everyone at that age, it became a kind of talisman; while the fascination lasted, I read it over and over, over and over, and always with the same freshness of interest. It was a romantic novel of derring-do in the wars between France and England in the Middle Ages, and DuGuesclin appeared in only one episode, where he was revealed sitting at the fireside of a wayside inn, cracking walnuts with his teeth and drinking wine.

I had no wine available, but I did my best to crack walnuts with my teeth, to the considerable distress of my mother. Later on, I was Whispering Smith, and, before that, a young fellow named Chip, of the "Flying U." Both were cowboys, characters in a series of Western novels, and both were quiet, innocent-seeming, soft-spoken, but deadly underneath. I can still hear my father's exasperated, "What's the matter with the boy, anyway? I can't hear a word he's saying. Speak up, Bob!" when I was being Whispering Smith.

Still later, I blinked, and that again was a cause of bewilderment and concern to my parents. "Do you suppose there's anything wrong with his eyes, and we ought to take him to a doctor?" I heard my mother asking one night. "He reads so much!"

"Well, I read a lot, too. But it hasn't hurt my eyes," said my father.

"You both read too much," said my mother, with conviction. She was far too active and intense a person to waste much time on books, and she was convinced that poring over them was somehow harmful. "Is it the light?" she asked, turning to me.

"I'm all *right!*" I told her disgustedly. And I was; I was merely being Mr. Marston, my high-school English teacher at the time, and Mr. Marston was unique in my experience in that he not only taught English composition, but he also wrote, and sold things, himself. The things he wrote were mainly squibs and short humorous pieces for *Judge*, *Puck*, and the old *Life*, but he was the first real, practicing writer I had ever encountered, and I was deeply in awe of him. And Mr. Marston, a short, dapper, worldly man (he was even supposed to be writing a play), had a way of blinking, especially when he was trying to emphasize a point and talking earnestly. I blinked, too, I suppose on the off-chance that it was part of whatever personal magic he had that had helped raise him to his present eminence—and if that were the case, I'd be a fool not to try it, too.

It is a kind of magic, this business of identification, and it occurs most powerfully in youth, when the whole world seems magical anyway, and full of mysterious hints and promises. I "identified" with Mr. Marston, although even then I half knew he was a bit superficial and given to name-dropping and so on. Oddly, though, possibly because I was older, I never took out after even my favorite teachers in college—like—Johnny Berdan (his pipes), Billy Phelps (his bonhommie), Chauncey Tinker (his tall shyness), although actually, and with reason, I admired them more.

To be sure, too, the quality, and the efficacy of the magic

varies according to circumstances. Dried wasps' eyes, popular as an aphrodisiac in India, act differently on different persons, and this I think is somehow related to that small, thin, deeply hidden but intractable core that represents the individual's basic personality, the tiny ego—ego, per se—that he is born with, and that will forever make him a little different from everyone else and so, unalterably, an identity.

I didn't stay with Wolf Larsen long, because there was something alien in him, something outside me. I was more the Chip or the Whispering Smith sort; what appealed to me was the quiet, unassuming stranger who sat at a corner table in the Malamute Saloon, drinking root beer or some such innocuous beverage, and who only went into action when the big, tough "hard cases" at the bar began to bully him.

Yet it seems that some of the threads remain, long, long, in one's nature, and possibly forever, subject to change, perhaps, but never to total extinction. After all, I did find myself in a Wolf Larsen mood only recently, and after all those years; and when, a short time ago, in Jay Williams's novel *The Siege*, I came across a curly-haired, angelic-looking young knight named Amauric de Montjoie (as frail as my old friend Chip, and just as lethal), I felt a touch of the old affinity. I was still holding down that corner table, along with Amauric de Montjoie this time, and those loud-mouthed ruffians at the bar had better think twice before they tackled us!

Indeed, the more I think of it, the more I wonder. Who was that young man, for instance, who came from France on the liner *Paris*, in the late fall of 1927? His name was Coates, according to his passport, but surely he was not the same Coates who had gone abroad some five years earlier.

The first was dressed pretty much in what was then (but, thank God, was not called) the "Ivy League" fashion: shirt with buttoned-down collar, suit with unlined three-button jacket, wool socks, wing-tipped oxfords, and, of course, with the face clean-shaven.

The new one was mustached and bearded and hatless. (The old one had worn a felt hat, properly crumpled, as his one deviation from neatness and propriety.) His jacket was determinedly different from his pants, and his shirt was a French workman's blue flannel one, worn tieless and open at the throat: his shoes were the heavy French workman's. Incongruously (though at the time he didn't realize this), he was carrying a walking stick.

The beard and mustache lasted only a week or two; and the clothes changed gradually. But the walking stick I carried longer; and there were other, more subtle little mannerisms—evidence, also, of my lost cosmopolitan past—that I hung onto even longer. It was years, for example, before I could bring myself to discard the crossed French 7, and even longer still before I omitted the comma that the French always put between the house number and the name of the street in writing an address.

But then, how about the people who, having once taken their car abroad, forget for years to take off the oval "GB" plate which shows they have been in England?

Who am I, anyway?

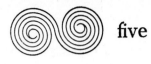 five

If life is difficult to understand, death is a matter so vast that
I imagine no one grasps its meaning completely until the
moment when it encloses him. In most cases, I think, comprehension comes slowly, gradually, piecemeal; certainly
it has been so this far in my own life. I remember the first
time I saw death, immediate and close at hand. It was when
my family was living in Rochester, and I was about fifteen.
I was walking on one of the streets in our quiet neighborhood—Kislingbury, maybe, or Selye Terrace—one summer afternoon when a car came up behind me and passed
me, traveling fairly fast. As it reached the corner ahead,
an old man on a bicycle rode out square in front of it.

The rest happened in an instant, and there was not a
chance of anyone's avoiding it. There was a thud and crash
of glass, metal, and, probably, flesh, meeting, mingling,
and smashing, and then, even as the car slid and skidded, I
saw the man hurled back and down, disappearing in front
of the car's black bulk, and the bicycle ground under one
front wheel and shot out sidewise.

By the time I ran up, the car's driver—a big, red-faced,
prosperous-looking man in a light gray suit ("Damn it,

damn it, *damn* it!" he was crying, and "He was on the wrong side of the *street!*")—was out and running to the front of the car. By then, others were coming, too—a man who had been mowing a lawn up near the corner, and a couple of men who had been walking on the sidewalk opposite—while from the until-then drowsing houses, still others were appearing: women in their house dresses coming to the doors or out onto the porches, men hurrying around from the back yards. The whole neighborhood was awakening to the fact that there had been an accident.

Meantime, the man lay sprawled on the pavement, dead, to all appearances. He was small and thin, as I remember him—small and thin with the wizenedness that comes with age—lank-faced and white-haired, wearing a pair of brown pants and a clean white shirt, short-sleeved, that revealed the skinniness of his arms; and he wasn't dead, really. He lay there motionless for what seemed like a number of minutes, while one woman went to get blankets and another to telephone for an ambulance, and then suddenly he stirred, and the pale lips moved.

"Oh dear. Oh dear. Oh dear," he began muttering softly. He was bruised, and there were cuts on one arm and on his cheek, from which he was bleeding. But, by a miracle, he seemed otherwise uninjured. A little later, he was struggling to sit up, and, when they made him lie still, feeling feebly about for his glasses, which lay smashed beside him.

"But I've got to get back!" he protested. "Can't you see? I've got to get *back!*"

But he *had* been dead, as far as I was concerned—as, in a queer way, those few seconds between the time he came wobbling out of the side street and the moment he landed on the pavement had been his whole life for me. He was old, really old; I was far too young then to be a sure judge of age, but I imagine he must have been in his seventies, or close to them, and, like most old men, probably absent-minded into the bargain. Unsteady, too; he had no business being on a bicycle in the first place.

No doubt his family—the married daughter he lived with, maybe, and her husband—had been urging him all along to give the thing up, quit riding it. "The stores will deliver anything you want, Pa, or one of the kids can get it," they'd told him. "And Joe or I will take you riding in the car any time you want to."

But the old man was stubborn, and a relic of the fast-disappearing bicycling generation besides, so he probably set great store by his bicycle. ("Where's my wheel?" he'd demanded once, as he was reviving, and the old-fashioned term—which my father still used, incidentally—had pointed up his age still further. "I don't want anything to happen to that wheel.") Had he belonged, as my father had, to one of those sporty "century clubs," whose members could boast that they'd covered a round hundred miles or more in the space of twenty-four hours on a wheel?

In any case, he had probably resisted all the family's pleadings. "I can take care of myself, don't you fear," he had told them every time the subject came up; and when they thought about it, really, nothing *had* ever happened to him, and it was a relief to have him out of the house occasionally. This time, possibly, he'd been riding over to Maplewood Park, to tour the quiet paths and drives there.

I stayed, watching, till the ambulance came, and then I went on my way. Whatever happened to him, it was fairly clear that his bicycling days were over.

The old man had been dead—for me, anyway—long enough to show me the simple fact of death's suddenness. It was winter, on a cold, clear, moonless night, and I was coming home, late, from the Kondolfs' pond up on Seneca Parkway, where my friends and I skated in season, when an understanding of death's finality was borne in on me.

In a way, it was nothing, really. But an uncle of mine, Uncle Will Davidson, had died a few months earlier, and I had been to the funeral and had seen him in his coffin. He had been my favorite uncle. The youngest of my mother's several brothers and sisters, he had also been the gayest, and he had played with me untiringly, joked with me, teasing, cajoling, from as far back as I could remember.

His playful moods always came without warning, and because I was an only child, they were especially delightful to me. I could never tell when some fancy would seize him, and, when it did, it might range anywhere from a game of giveaway checkers, with all the rules turned topsy-turvy, to a game of cowboy and bandit, with the two of us bang-banging away at each other wildly from behind the sofas and chairs in the living room.

He accepted the sometimes equally unexpected results of his joking. Once, when I was a small youngster (by the time a few years had passed, the episode had become a family anecdote, repeated endlessly, to, of course, my own embarrassment), he was sitting opposite me at table, smoking. Suddenly I heard him cry out, "Bob! Bob! I'm on fire!" and I turned to see his whole face—or his mouth and nostrils, anyway—enveloped in smoke.

He had simply held his breath and let a mouthful of smoke trickle slowly out. But without a moment's hesitation, and with what I still think was admirable presence of mind, I seized a glass of water and dashed it in his face. To his credit, Uncle Will laughed as heartily as the rest of the family.

And now I had been to his funeral; I had seen him in his

coffin. Yet it was not until that starry winter's night months later that the full realization came over me—and with no pain or anguish that I can remember, either, but, rather, with a feeling of awe at the finality of it—that Uncle Will was dead, really dead; I would never see him, hear him, *have* him again.

I can't tell, now, why the feeling came at me at just that moment. I suppose it must have sprung from some glancing realization that I was looking straight into infinity itself when I looked up at the sky, though I doubt if I even figured out that much of it then.

But I can still see the flat, snowy areas of that semisuburban section, then only scatteredly built up with houses; feel the cold—the biting, nose-piercing cold that the Lake cities know; see the sky, ice-black where it wasn't glittering; and feel, too, though more dimly now, the force of that instant of realization: that my uncle was dead, dead for good, for ever.

And there was a late fall day—warm, smoky, hazy, lazy, the lawns littered with leaves and the gutters piled high with them, and some of the piles burning cracklingly while a householder watched and tended—when I was walking again in Rochester, this time on Emerson Street, and a sense of what I can only think of as death's immensity was brought home to me. I was passing a sort of exercise hall, or riding arena—a long, low-roofed building set back a little way from the street; it was a building that had always held a fascination for me, since it was the place where Rochester's fashionable cavalry unit, Squadron A of the National Guard, an organization I longed to belong to some day, held its drills. And now, on the stretch of lawn before it, there was a group of youngsters running about, more or less at random, in a game of touch football.

Suddenly, the neighborhood scene, ordinary and innocent as it was, coalesced into sadness, and I thought, These trees, these buildings—that old telephone pole, even—will all still be here when I'm dead and gone.

The thing I remember most clearly about the moment was the feeling I had of complete isolation, a kind of cosmic loneliness. I was about sixteen at the time, and that is always an age of uncertainty, when one is no longer a boy and still not yet in any degree a man.

Perhaps, unconsciously, my sense of the situation may have been heightened by the contrast before me: on the one hand, the boys, just young enough for me to feel superior to them (while possibly envying their noisy romping), and, on the other, the riding hall, the symbol of the kind of manly adventure that was unattainable as yet to me, which I envied, too.

And it was all overblown, in the very fashion of the sixteen-year-old. But it was my first real intimation of my own mortality, and so, to me, memorable, and I still recall that there was no rancor or bitterness about it; rather, it was a feeling almost of tenderness—tolerant and all-enveloping, full of kinship and resignation—toward everyone and everything, these things that would remain after I had vanished. It may be through just such experiences that the process of growing up occurs.

It was summer again, vacation time, and I had a vacation job at the Eastman Kodak plant, out on Lake Avenue, when I realized death's arbitrariness, its capriciousness.

This was my first real job, for before that all I had done was to run a newspaper route or do errands for the corner grocery—kid stuff, obviously—while now I was working with men, at one part, at least, of men's occupations. I worked in the factory "yard," as it was called, first as a sort of general handyman, digging ditches, loading and unloading freight cars, and so on, and then (promoted, in a sense) as a helper to the yard drayman, Frank Tobin.

Mr. Tobin was fairly well on in years by the time I encountered him—past sixty, I'd say, though, as I've said earlier, a boy's idea of age is unreliable—but still solidly built and quite handy in his movements, grave, quiet, and with a certain natural dignity of manner. He was one of those men who, on aging, seem to get grayer all over; not only his hair and mustache, but the very flesh of his face seemed to have lost color, settling to a uniform grayish tinge that was matched by the dusty work shirt and pants that were his usual costume.

I had been told that he was a little hard to get along with —he didn't mingle much with the others about the yard, for one thing—so I was a little scared of him to begin with. Certainly when the yard foreman stopped him as he was driving along one Monday morning and introduced me, he seemed almost monumental in his gray, graven solemnity, sitting staring down at me with his heavy-lidded brown eyes, the reins slack in his hands, and his body hunched a little on the wagon seat.

"College kid?" he asked, I remember, not of me, though he was looking at me, but of the foreman.

"No. High-school," the foreman told him.

Mr. Tobin drew the side of his hand across his chin in what I was to learn was one of his habitual gestures, and sighed, not sadly or in any other way, just noncommittally. "Hop in, boy," he said.

I climbed up to sit on the worn black leather cushion beside him, and we were off. It was not a particularly auspicious beginning, obviously, but, for all that, the next few weeks, when I was working with him, were among the pleasantest that I remember.

Part of it was because of a gift Mr. Tobin had—tact, I guess, is the word that would sum it up—for silence when silence was appropriate, and for speech when that was demanded. So, that first day, he said nothing for quite a while, and neither did I. To tell the truth, I was at once intimidated and annoyed by the man. (After all, that "kid"! That "high-school"!) But when he spoke at last, it turned out that my silence, grim as it had been on my part, had actually pleased him.

"Well, at least you don't talk a man's arm off," he said morosely, then went on. He had a way of talking in broken sentences.

"Some of those other kids I've had. That last one, the college kid before you. All he did was just talk, talk, talk, talk, all the time. Not about his studies. Oh, no! No mention of that! But about his boxing. And baseball. And what an athlete he was. And, of course, the girls. What high school d'you go to?" he asked, and I realized he had turned half around in his seat to squint at me.

When I told him West High, he even smiled a little. "My daughter went there. Elizabeth. She'd a been before your time, though. She's in college now. Nursing college," he added before I could ask what one. "She's getting the education that was denied her mother and me.

"Here we are, then," he said as he pulled up alongside a big lumber pile by the freight siding. "Let's see how good you are at handing up two-by-fours." And with a remarkable agility for a man of his weight, he jumped down from his side of the wagon.

I don't want to go on too long about Mr. Tobin. He's gone—he was doomed, even then, though of course neither he nor I knew it. But for some reason I can't quite define—perhaps simply because, outside my family, he was the first grown man I'd ever been in such close day-by-day relationship with—he made a deep impression on me, and I'd like to pay him some tribute now.

If I have made him seem gruff, he was so only superficially, and he soon came to hold an almost paternal interest in me and my doings. He was North Country Irish, an Ulsterman, and, as is true of all such, his basic mood was a little dour. But he could liven up on occasion, and his early stiffness with me soon vanished, transformed into an easygoing loquacity that was actually a sort of soliloquizing; like that of a good many men who lead fairly solitary lives, his talk was frequently as much to himself as it was to me.

To be sure, this made him tend toward the oracular. But that didn't matter, either. The plain truth, I guess, is that I was drawn to Mr. Tobin, as I think he was to me, and the seat of a horse-drawn wagon is perhaps the best place for a friendly relationship such as ours was to develop.

I can still recall the easy atmosphere of those days, that summer, when we'd be ambling along unhurriedly on some job about the plant, or, better still, on some longer, even more leisurely errand that took us through the shady streets outside, talking ramblingly or not talking, listening or not listening—and all this to the grate of the wheels and the creak and strain of the harness, and with the brown rumps of the horses heaving, swaying, settling, in unison, and then heaving again, as they plodded along before us.

Mr. Tobin talked often of his wife, and so fondly that I began almost to feel that I knew her. At least I got to the point where I could picture her. I saw her as a short, plump, pleasant-faced, capable woman, Scotch-Irish ("But not one of your raw-boned, big-footed ones. She's in fact a little on the small side. But, Lord! Can she run a house for you! And neat, too. Neat as a pin!")—and when I did meet her, once, she was almost exactly as I had imagined her.

The one time I met her was on a Saturday night in downtown Rochester, on West Main Street—but that is another part of the story of my acquaintance with Mr. Tobin. He had his problems. He fretted a good deal about his daughter, for one thing; she was engaged to a young man he didn't like, and he was afraid she would "mess up her life" if she married him. More immediately, he had bought a new suit, and that had led him into difficulties.

Ordinarily, I gathered, his wife went along and took charge of such purchases for him. This time, though, it was for his daughter's birthday party, and some rebellious instinct had stirred within him. He had bought the suit himself, and the result had been disastrous.

"They made the sleeves too short; they made the pants too short," he told me. "They just ruined it! And the trouble is, without Mamie along I didn't notice. She's the one that takes charge of such things."

I was surprised at his making so much of what seemed to be a simple matter. But I was learning—and this from Mr. Tobin, too—that age alone does not make a man invulnerable; grown people, I was discovering, had their weaknesses, too.

"Well, good heavens, then, take it back," I told him. "They ought to make it right."

He had bought the suit at a shop called McFarlin's, and when I added that I'd bought clothes there myself, he glanced at me with a momentary flash of hope. Then he shook his head; that salesman, whoever he was, had really awed him. "No. What you don't see, boy, the trouble is that I had the try-on. I accepted the blamed thing. I accepted it."

"Well, take it to a tailor, then. Have him fix it." But that went against the grain, too, for, to tell the truth, Mr. Tobin was a little close about money. "Or," I added, "why not take your wife along to the store? I'll bet she can handle it."

Almost instantly, I realized that this was the advice he had been waiting for. To be sure, he demurred a little. "But that takes away from the surprise," he protested. "She's not supposed to see it before the party."

"Better that than surprising her with a suit that doesn't fit," I countered, and he finally agreed.

I saw him the following Saturday evening, with his wife, in the downtown crowds. Mr. Tobin had a slow, thrusting, rather ponderous walk, and as I see him now, in recollection, he was like some great ship, pushing his way in my direction. He was beaming.

"It's all right!" he cried, and hesitated only an instant. "Young fellow," he added. I was with another boy and a couple of girls, and I was glad, and grateful, that he hadn't used his customary "boy."

"Thanks to you, and the wife, too," he went on. "They said they'd fix that suit up right away. Guess they didn't dare try to talk Mamie down!" And they passed me, she nodding and smiling, he grinning broadly, and we went our separate ways. We four were headed, as I remember, for Odenbach's Rathskeller, a rather sporty place to take a girl in those days.

And that, indeed, was the last time I saw Mr. Tobin, for he died in his sleep that same night, of a heart attack, and when I turned up for work the next Monday, it was the foreman, a wiry, black-haired Italian whose name I forget, who told me.

"Yeah, too bad," he said before I could even comment. "You and him got along good, too, didn't you?" He stood for a few seconds in silence, staring gravely at the ground in deference to the sad occasion. "And I know how you feel, kid," he went on, and he patted my arm.

As a matter of fact, I can't recall feeling anything at the moment; the event was too sudden—or, as I said earlier, too arbitrary, too capricious—for me to grasp immediately. "But you know," he went on, "when you come to think of it, at his age, too, it's the best way to go. Like that," and he snapped his fingers. "After all, it comes to all of us."

That, I guess, was Mr. Tobin's epitaph. But my feeling at the time—and I'm not so sure it was entirely a childish one—was that it was just too darned bad that he wasn't going to get any pleasure out of that new suit.

I sometimes think that death, or our appreciation of it, comes in waves. There is the first one—so small that it's hardly noticeable, because we ourselves are so young—in which the grandparents and the older relatives are involved; the second, a little larger, is the one involving parents, and the people of their generation; larger still is the one of our own friends and close contemporaries; and then, finally, inevitably, comes the last one, engulfing everything.

It occurs to me, though, that it's odd that so many of my recollections on so portentous a subject should center on Rochester. For Rochester to me was a happy time, a time of growing up into all sorts of knowledges, from the starting to learn about girls to the beginning feeling of one's own aspirations and capabilities. (And is death, the antithesis, somewhere concealed in the process?)

At any rate, even the clothing store, McFarlin's, has its cheerful connotations in my mind. It was a small store—

small, at least, compared with Sibley, Watson and Curr and some of the others in Rochester—but someone in the management that year had had the novel notion of giving away, free, a monocle with each young man's suit that was purchased. The monocles were of plain glass, of course, but with a neat-looking thin black frame and a cord attached, and for a while they created what amounted to a run on the store.

Anyone who had any influence at all with his parents got a new suit at McFarlin's, just to get the monocle; and while the vogue lasted, we wore them everywhere—furtively at school, till the teachers shut down on us completely, and more openly at games, parties, and other gatherings.

In fact, one afternoon in the fall, not long after Mr. Tobin's death, a group of us skipped school and, young bloods that we were, went down to the old Columbia Burlesque Theatre and sat, wearing our monocles, lined up in the very first row. As it turned out, we almost broke up the show, for when the girls of the chorus came out in the opening number and saw us, they got to laughing so hard that the manager had to ring down the curtain, weed out our monocles, and then start things all over again.

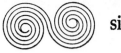 six

Whenever I run across an article about juvenile delin-
quents—and, as everyone knows, these appear fairly frequently nowadays—I am likely to have a twinge of fellow
feeling for the poor youngsters involved. There was a time
—still vivid in my mind, too—when I came close to being
a juvenile delinquent myself. That was years ago, when
I was living in Rochester, and it all began late one summer
afternoon on the playground of the old Dewey Avenue
School, not far from my parents' home, on Bryan Street.

I wasn't going to that particular school at the time; I was,
in fact, in my second year at West High School over on
the other side of town. And I have mentioned this school
and that general period earlier. But I think now I might
describe it a little more in detail. Anyway, the big, old-
fashioned school, three stories high, built of red brick, and
rambling, had a playground to match its size. Two blocks
long on each side, the playground had room for football
or, interchangeably, soccer or baseball; it had a couple of
tennis courts, too, as well as swings, teeter-totters, and such
like for younger children. As I've also said earlier, that sum-

mer—indeed, that whole year—a group of us older boys had more or less taken it over.

I can't recall now quite how that happened, if indeed I ever did know, for I was new in the neighborhood. It may have been the outgrowth of a vogue for tennis we all had at that period that drew us to the courts there; it may have been a kind of culmination of those wayward, mysterious impulses that drive boys in their early and middle teens to form coteries—tight, clannish, partly clandestine, and as ephemeral, usually, as the boys themselves think them to be everlasting. Partly, certainly, it was due to the heady feeling the move up from grade school to high school had given us; we were well on our way to being men now, we thought, and were automatically entitled to lord it over the lesser fellows.

At all events, some eight or nine of us—Charlie Bowman, Paul Benedict, Bill Ingle, Wallie Blaine (these are some of the names that come back to me at the moment)—really "owned" the playground that summer. There was no such thing as a playground director in those simple days. Old Mr. Roach, the school janitor—a gray, spidery, taciturn Ulsterman—was supposed, I believe, to be technically in charge.

But he was never a man to overexert himself, and, besides, it was summer, and hence, in some sense, a vacation time for him, too; about all he did was to put out the tennis nets and the rest of the playground equipment in the morning and leave a door open into the cellar for us to put them away at night. Otherwise, we were pretty much untrammeled; we ran the younger kids' baseball games, bossed their other activities, and, pre-empting the courts without question, played tennis, tennis endlessly.

We'd play mornings and afternoons, and—in the summer at least and if there was nothing else impending—we would usually be back in the early evening again. Summer days in Rochester's latitude are long, and the onset of evening is gradual: we lingered, too, playing games of cross tag that lapsed in the middle or veered into horseplay, or just lying on the grassy ground and talking.

There was a clump of young trees at one edge of the tennis courts, more or less in the middle of the area, where we usually gathered; otherwise, the playground was fairly barren, all turf and trodden earth. But its very size made it seem almost parklike, and this gave it a certain feeling of isolation, too. Facing it, all around, were the neat two-story homes that were typical of that part of Rochester, shingled or clapboarded, each with its concrete driveway leading back to the garage at the rear, its stretch of lawn and its clump of arborvitae, its dormered roof and wide, shadowy porch, and with now, as the evening deepened, its downstairs windows—hall, dining-room, living-room, kitchen—being lighted.

They were our homes, or if they were not ours in actuality, ours being on different streets here and there in the neighborhood, they were ours in essence, and we knew well enough what went on inside them—the daughter playing the phonograph, perhaps, while the father sat reading, the mother out in the kitchen, putting dishes away or readying things for tomorrow's breakfast.

But their distance gave them a look of unreality and us a feeling of remoteness; they were the far façade of a different world, the world of grownups and family, and, familiar and pleasant as that world was—and comfortable, too—we lingered still on the playground, putting off the moment when by merely running up a few short steps and opening a door we would be plunged back into it.

I don't think our parents minded our haunting the playground in the way we did. For one thing, I suppose they felt at least that they "knew where we were." If any of them decided suddenly on some project for the evening—the movies, perhaps, or just a drive out to Lake Ontario (in that gentler time, when traffic was no problem and the motorcar still something of an adventure, people often made little evening excursions like that)—they would drive up to the curb by the playground, sound their horn, and wait till the son, recognizing the family car, ran down to join them.

So it was all very innocent, and even a little silly. I remember once when one of the fellows—Bill Ingle, I think it was—found out from some recondite source that when a group of men dropped into one of the hotel bars downtown it was the customary thing for one of the gentlemen to "stand treat" for the others, after which one or two of the others would follow suit. Our only "bar" was Mr. Heinzelmann's candy store and soda fountain, about a block farther up Dewey Avenue from the playground, and in the afternoons especially we usually repaired there for an ice-cream soda or some such, to sustain us in the half-hour or so before dinner.

We did our best to fit in with grown-up procedure, however, and for a while whatever imps of perversity there are must have had a jolly time of it looking down at us lolling negligently at Mr. Heinzelmann's marble-topped fountain counter—true men of the world, every inch of us—and "standing treat" in the adult fashion.

All this, certainly, must have delighted Mr. Heinzelmann, however much it may have puzzled him, too. But it ended fairly abruptly—partly because of the wear and tear on our allowances, but I think rather more because our parents, seeing us come reeling home, no longer ravenous but, instead, so full of a mixture of hot-fudge sundaes, banana splits, and pineapple sundaes that we could hardly move, began investigating.

Our trouble was, I guess, that we hadn't yet learned that mixing drinks of any category is likely to be dangerous.

Yet it has only now struck me that, except for our innocence, and the protection our middle-class background gave us from any contact with real criminality, we were actually a "gang," or we had the makings of one—as, one night, to our own surprise, we discovered.

That was when we raided the Boy Scout camp, and this began one afternoon when Wallie Blaine mentioned, possibly a bit self-importantly, that he had to go home early; he was camping out with his troop that night. Even then, everything would have been all right if it hadn't been Wallie who said it.

Wallie, short, fat, and bumbling, and just pettish enough to give spice to the sport of tormenting him, was not so much a member of our group as the butt of it. I don't think we'd known he was a Boy Scout till then, and the picture of him—at his age, too, for we felt that we'd all outgrown such childish pursuits—still running around in a scarf and sombrero, khaki shorts and blouse with a knapsack over his shoulder, was to us anyway, irresistible.

We kidded him about it, if the kind of heavy-handed verbal mauling boys of that age go in for can be called kidding.

"Gee, Wallie! Aren't you scared? Suppose the tent falls in!"

"It won't. I thought everybody knew how to pitch a tent."

And he told us that the rest of the boys in the troop were young; he was a kind of assistant to the Scoutmaster.

"What do you do when they want to go to the bathroom, Wallie?" we asked. "Do you have to go with them?"

Even after he'd left—in a huff, of course—the idea of Wallie in a Boy Scout troop, and our sallies about it, still convulsed us, and before we went home for dinner, we had decided to go out that evening and take a look at Wallie's encampment.

That's a simple statement, on the face of it, and yet there is a mystery about it; even now, in my mind, it's hard to reconcile such an excursion with the usual round of our life that summer. For if the playground was, in a way, our escape, it was also our tether. More than that, the neighborhood enclosed us, and so did our age, and our age's inclinations.

Later, just a year or so later, we were to be bored with tennis, and our tight tribal feeling would be beginning to evaporate, too. Girls would occupy us more by that time, and, borrowing a family car, we'd be taking them on wider excursions, making foursomes to go to the band concerts in Maplewood Park, or the roller-coaster rides at Sea Breeze, out at the lake front—and then driving home slowly, tentatively amorous, through the cool, pale, moonlit evenings.

This, though, was the farthest we'd ever wandered afield until then, and I can only explain it as a step in a new direction. It was a gesture of revolt, perhaps—for I'm sure none of us told his parents where he was going—and a venturing toward independence, manliness, too; it was the beginning of a change.

We went out, anyway, on the Dewey Avenue trolley, for Wallie, poor fellow, had even told us where the camp was to be—on a farm a half-mile or so outside town, beyond the trolley-line terminus. The odd thing, too, is that the farther we went, the more ganglike we became. We skylarked on the trolley till the passengers glared; and when we came to the little settlement on the Ridge Road, at the terminus, we marched through it yelling and singing—singing, I'm afraid, nothing more desperate than our own West High School songs.

Approaching the farm, though, we quieted; and as we sighted the camp at last—a ring of pup tents in a hollow, some aglow, paper-lantern-like, with a lamp inside, some still canvas-white and ghostly, and with a bonfire at the center of the circle—it was by common unspoken agreement that we dropped back and then, cautiously, at first crouching and finally on our hands and knees, began working our way across the field on the small bluff above.

We had been an ordinary group of boys at the playground, a gang on the trolley; now we were sharpshooters reconnoitering the enemy, and when we got to the edge of the field and could look down on the scene below—a few boys, Wallie among them, sitting around the campfire, others washing their mess kits in the stream that flowed through the hollow or moving about here and there —I think we all had a taste of that tight, secret pleasure spies must have, of being the all-seeing, unsuspected witnesses, observing but unobserved.

A moment later, we were Indians as—again, as far as I can recall, on a common impulse—we jumped up and ran shrieking down upon them.

Even now, our intentions, if a bit scatterbrained, were innocent. We were showing off, of course, and surely we did hope to startle them. But we felt that somehow, beyond all our shouting and so on, we'd be known, we'd be *rec-*

ognized—as on our wildest Halloween escapades, for example, beneath our most fantastic disguises, we were recognized in our own neighborhood as just boys on a rampage, and harmless.

This time, though, we weren't. We were outside our neighborhood, to begin with; more than that, we hadn't considered the suddenness of our onslaught and its effect on a bunch of small boys camping out in the lonely dark of the countryside. Nor, I must add, had we counted on the timidity of the Scoutmaster.

What ensued, anyway, went far beyond anything we could have expected. There was an instant's hush as we burst in, and a startled staring—and then turmoil and confusion, and on such a scale that I can remember it only glancingly: a boy's face flaring up at mine and then vanishing, and behind him a tent going down and then another; a crisscrossing of flashlight beams and a frantic yelling; figures leaping and darting across the light of the fire and then past it into the darkness; and then silence and emptiness, in which we were left—aghast, now, ourselves, at the havoc we'd wrought—calling plaintively, "Wallie! Wallie!" out into the deepening night. "Listen, Wallie, it's just us!"

In a minute or two, they all came straggling back.

But our adventures were not over yet; instead, from then on, trouble piled on trouble. The boys forgave us at once; indeed—boys are elastic at that age—the whole episode only added a touch of novelty to their night outdoors. The Scoutmaster, though, took a darker view of the proceedings. He was a sandy-haired, pale, rather scrawny man, as I remember him, and we figured he must have run farther than the rest at our onslaught, for he was the last to

return. When he did, it was to order us off the place immediately.

He was quite justified in that, of course; without meaning to, we had acted like a bunch of young ruffians. What
he failed to tell us was that when *he* had run away, he had
made a good job of it. He had run all the way to the farmhouse on the property and had phoned the Rochester
police, and the farmer, pending their arrival, had offered
to round up some friends, in a kind of makeshift posse, to
come to the rescue meanwhile. We didn't know—we
didn't even suspect—what a chain of alarm we had waked,
out there in the country evening, until, shuffling off down
the road, depressed and considerably chastened, we ran
head on into the posse, coming toward us.

All this happened, as I've said, years ago, and I find that,
in my own mind, at least, distant memories such as this
tend to fall into separate episodes, each one vivid in itself
but pretty much isolated, so that the whole experience is,
so to speak, skeletonized into a series of dramatic but
largely unrelated flashes.

Thus, I can recall—in that odd, oblique way in which
one figures both as an observer and as a participant—our
long, lazy evenings on the playground; I can see us marching through the village street, with its scattering of white-
painted houses; and I can see, and feel, too, the excitement
and tension of our charge down on the encampment.

Even more clearly still, I can recall the look of that group
of men, dark, hostile—most of all, anonymous—bunched
against the white gravel road, as they advanced upon us.
What they'd expected to find themselves up against I have
no way of knowing, but they had obviously prepared for
the worst, because one man had a shotgun and a couple
had clubs, and another actually had a pitchfork; it was the

pitchfork that scared me most. And it occurs to me, now, that quite possibly they were as frightened as we were, for when a voice came out of the group—"Stop right where you are, now!" it called—it was a little shaky. We didn't stop; we just cut and ran.

After that, it was everyone for himself. I remember racing across fields and scrambling, stumbling, over fences. In the next scene—the next of any clarity, that is—I am walking along the Ridge Road. I have somehow joined forces with another boy—as I recall it, it's Bill Ingle—and if we had been part of a gang earlier, it was a gang long since dispersed; if we were hoodlums once, we are now singularly dispirited ones, and lost, too, at least in the sense that we daren't go back through the village to the trolley line, and have no idea how we are going to make our way home in any other fashion.

We were waifs, really, Bill and I, and it was late by then, really late, and dark. When a car came up behind us and, instead of passing, stopped, with its headlights full upon— well, we felt, or I did, anyway, that the ultimate doom was upon us.

We made a jump, instinctively, for the side of the road. But as we did so, a spotlight caught us, and a man cried, "Stop!" We stopped. A moment later, the car was beside us. It was a police car, all right—we could tell that by the uniform of the driver. But the man who leaned out from the seat beside him was in plain clothes—a neat blue suit and a straw hat tipped well back from a round, cheerful face. It may have been some psychological reaction on my part, but he looked surprisingly like my father, and his voice was, equally surprisingly, friendly.

"Where you heading for, kids?" he demanded—and we told him, into the city.

"Yeah, but where?" And I said Bryan Street. Bill Ingle, I suppose, said Hollis Avenue. The man studied us for a moment. He seemed to be in no hurry to get out the handcuffs.

"Well, climb in, then," he said, and he reached back to unlatch the rear door. "We're going that way ourselves. Give you a lift." We got in. What else was there to do?

"How'd you get out here, anyway?" he asked next. (Though I can't remember his exact words, I can recall the sense of them.)

"We were walking."

"Kind of a long walk, wasn't it?" he said, and we answered, truthfully, yes. "Funny thing," he went on after that. "We had a call from out around here, to Police Headquarters. From a Boy Scout camp. Seems the camp was raided." The man twisted around in his seat to look at us. "You wouldn't know anything about that, I suppose?"

Oh, no, sir, we told him. I think we felt, even then, that he knew all there was to know about us, but it seemed the only way to answer. Anyway, he seemed to accept it. "I guess not," he went on, nodding comfortably. "These were real roughnecks, from what they tell me—not your kind of fellows at all. Broke the camp up." We stiffened. "Tore the tents down. Beat the kids up—little kids, too," he went on, in his placid recital, while Bill and I looked at each other. "And to top that off, know what they did? They stole the Scoutmaster's watch and wallet!"

"That's not so!" Bill cried, and I hope I echoed him.

The man turned around farther in his seat and gazed at us. "Oh?" he said.

We, of course, were quaking. We had given ourselves away, at last. The man—he had already told us he was a detective—seemed not to notice. "Well, you know," he went on, "it turns out you're right. Seems the Scoutmaster lost his head, sort of, in the excitement, and forgot where he'd put the blamed things. But they turned up all right; they were under his pillow, in the end. There was a fellow out there—Walter, Wallie, Wallie something—said he knew the fellows. Funny, you being out here, right in the neighborhood, with all this going on, and not knowing anything about it. Do you know Wallie Blaine?" he de-manded.

"Yes," I said. "Well, yes, in a way."

He nodded. "Well, you know, it's a good thing to stay out of things like that. You know, kids, even your age, old enough to know better, they get all steamed up once in a while. They get a little bit too big for their breeches. And then, the first thing you know, they're in a jam." The car had made a turn or two, and then had driven straight away; we were in familiar territory now, going down Dewey Avenue. "Kids like you, even, kids of good families. Do your folks know where you are tonight?"

"No, sir."

"No? Why not? Were you visiting friends out there?"

"Well, we were going to. But—"

Again, he made no attempt to entrap us. "Sure," he said. The car had halted at the corner of Bryan. "You're near enough here, too, aren't you?" he asked Bill. "We'll let you both out here."

It was the time for a lecture if there ever was one. But, instead, he just sat there a moment, quietly looking at me. And by now the man's calm, and yet knowing, knowing, acquiescence in all our little deceptions had piled up in my mind till it had the ominous implications of a thundercloud.

Surely, surely—like a teacher trying to pry through our reticences, like any other of our grown-up inquisitors—

he would crack down on us now! And the fact that he didn't, that he let our small evasions lie like an open secret between us, gave a man-to-man atmosphere to our relations. He was treating us, really, like men, and in so doing, subtly, he had put a responsibility on us not to act like children any more. And then I—but I couldn't help it— reverted to the small-boy status.

"Did they catch any of the other fellows?" I asked.

"What other fellows?"

"The ones in the gang."

"Did I say anything about a gang?"

"Well, you know. I mean—"

"You mean the ones with the Boy Scouts and all that? That, a gang?" He turned to the driver, who snickered. And then, answering my question, "I wouldn't know. All I know is that we were the only car that went out there. So I guess the others must be walking home. Do 'em good, too," he added as the car drove away.

My last recollection of that long-ago evening is a little meager, and again it forms a picture at least partly out of context with the rest. I must have run the half-block or so to our house from where the police car had left me—the street dark and quiet, and the houses, set back on their neat individual lawns, beginning to go dark, too, or having only their bedroom windows lighted.

And I must have been scared, going up the front walk and up the porch steps, for in our house the downstairs windows were lit, as I'd known they'd be. My father and mother were waiting up for me; and, when they asked me where I had been, either from scaredness, or more likely in reaction to it—put simply, just the feeling of being safe home again—I came right out with the whole story.

My mother was horrified, particularly at the fact that

I'd been brought home in a police car, but my father took it more casually. Indeed, the clearest picture I have of that phase of the adventure is of him sitting in the high-backed old brown leather easy chair that he always sat in, in the space beside the bay window, with his opened book turned face down on his lap, looking back and forth between my mother and me, and laughing.

"Oh, he's all right," he told her. "Kids have got to cut loose once in a while. It's a sign that they're growing up." I remember his saying that (he had his store of stories about his own boyhood escapades), but I'm not sure now what it was he was laughing at—at the fiasco at the camp or the one in the road later, at the fact that the detective had looked like him, or just the fact that we'd felt impelled to embark on such an adventure. All I know is that, although his laughter piqued me a little, it was at the same time curiously reassuring, and in the end I found myself laughing, too.

 seven

I'd like to write about the old motorcars for a while, and for purely sentimental reasons. The first car that I, or, rather, my family owned, for I was only about sixteen at the time, was a Stoddard-Dayton, now an almost forgotten make, and there was something about the casual way we acquired it that was typical of the era—though here, perhaps, my father's own easygoing temperament may have had something to do with the situation.

This again was when we were living in Rochester, and the man who owned it was a friend, or at any rate an acquaintance, of a friend of my father's, which automatically placed him above suspicion; the deal went through so fast it must have made the man's head swim. I can't recall his name, but I can still see him clearly. He was a short, dapper man, brown-haired, brown-eyed, and brown-suited, with a manner at once brisk and affable. He was the salesman type, and he was clearly prepared for some brisk bargaining about the car; my father, though, soon cut him short.

"Is it in good shape?" he asked suddenly. I can only recall the broad details of the episode, but the man, I know, had been reciting the usual selling points—best of care, careful driving, low mileage; if it wasn't that he was moving out of town, he wouldn't think of selling, and so on—and my father's abrupt interruption brought him up short.

"Well," he said. "As I've just been telling you, all you have to do is look at the speedometer, under ten thousand. Or the tires—"

"Is it in good shape?" my father repeated. The man had driven us out into Maplewood Park, near his home and not far from ours, either, for a "demonstration," and we'd halted under the trees.

"I just put two new tires on this spring," the man said, running down a little. My father, I could see, was giving him his man-to-man look, where the eye meets eye and the truth must travel between them, and in spite of himself the man hesitated. "Yes," he said. "Well, yes. As far as I know, it's in pretty good shape."

The "as far as I know," I think, went down well with my father, who was still enough of a Yankee that he would never commit himself to an unqualified "yes" or "no" unless he was dead sure and rock certain of his ground. My father hesitated only an instant. Indeed—though I understand this quality in him better now than I did then—he couldn't, in pride, have waited longer. It was part of his own particular code of conduct that, the greater the sum involved, the more offhand he had to seem about it, and the price the man was asking was a round thousand dollars.

"Then we'll take it," he said.

"At the thousand?" the man asked quickly, and my father glanced at him.

"That's the price you mentioned, wasn't it?" he said. The man, a bit goggle-eyed, nodded.

That was all there was to it. And we owned a car, the car I'd been hungering for! Or if not quite that—for the one I'd really been dreaming of had been something more in the line of a National or a Marmon, the kind that ate up the track at the Indianapolis Speedway; or, failing that, something overpoweringly big and luxurious, like a Winton or a Lozier—I was old enough even then to realize that dreams of such magnitude rarely come true in their entirety. The point was that we owned a car—and, I must add, a good one, too, for my father's trustfulness turned out to be justified in this instance, and the little Stoddard-Dayton was a real honey in every way.

It was a rich, dark brown, which in itself was unusual in that period, when the standard color was black, and it was a racy-looking affair, too, in its own right. It had a "close-coupled" body, as they called the style then, which meant that it carried only four passengers, two in front and two in back, and the tonneau, instead of having the high, bosomy quality of the average touring car of the era, was comparatively low, streamlined, and narrow. It had a pair of big brass-trimmed acetylene headlights (electric lighting didn't come in until several years later), a fold-down windshield that made it seem even racier, and a business-like-looking, long-handled emergency brake lever jutting out beside the driver. I had coveted it, of course, from the moment I'd seen it. But I was at that intransigent age when all the adults around me seemed to be incurably foolish, inept, and wrong-minded; and until the magic words "we'll take it" had been spoken (and, I might add, I liked that "we," though my father was always generously tactful in that way), I hadn't been at all sure that he'd recognize what a prize he had before him, just for the grasping.

Now that it was ours, I was entranced with it—as I still am, over the years, to this day. To be sure, a slight complication arose when, on taking over the car—as we did, that same afternoon—my father and I had to confess that neither of us knew how to drive. But in those easy days of no license requirements, little traffic, and simple mechanisms, that was easily gotten over. It may seem incredible now, but the man and I simply changed places at the wheel—"Teach the boy," my father had said; partly, I believe, to gratify me and partly because he didn't want to be put in the position of taking lessons from a stranger—and right then and there, rather cursorily, I got my first and only driving lesson.

The man *was* in a hurry. He was, I truly believe, leaving town in a week or so, as he'd said he was, and now that the deal was consummated he had the true salesman's impulse to get the hell out of there before we changed our minds. But he showed me how to set the spark and gas levers (they stuck out on either side of the steering post, just beneath the wheel, and you set the spark back, or "retarded" it, and advanced the gas, for starting), how to shift the gears and so on, and he rode beside me watchfully while I practiced letting in the clutch and letting it out again, to get that all-important "feel" of it, as I guided the car slowly back and forth along the winding graveled drives of Maplewood Park. Then we drove him back to his own house and left him there. From then on, we were on our own.

We weren't such a menace to the highways, then or later, as it may seem. For one thing, I was conscientious: I wouldn't willingly have damaged a square inch of that car's paint, and, perhaps miraculously, I didn't. For another, the dangers were less; there were far fewer cars on the road to contend with, and in any case I spent a good many hours on our own quiet side streets, cautiously practicing, before attempting any more extended forays.

In a sense, too, it was all part of the innocence of that era.

We learned pretty much everything by trial and error in those days. Last summer, at the sports-car races at Thompson, Connecticut, I heard a racing driver explain how a man, if he's clever enough, can change gears without declutching, and in the midst of it I was reminded how, almost by accident, I had done the same thing years ago in our old Stoddard-Dayton.

That was when our clutch pedal broke, and it happened only a month or so, at most, after we'd bought the car.

It was also the first time I'd ever driven the car at night, and the night, in such circumstances, can be portentous. I was driving some high-school friends of mine home, and we'd just started across Dewey Avenue, near our house, when I saw a trolley car approaching. I jammed both clutch and brake pedals down, and the clutch pedal gave way; the engine stalled, of course—and there we were, stalled too, and in the middle of the car track.

I can still see that trolley car, its motorman invisible and hence unpredictable behind the glare of the searchlight, bearing down upon us. There was a moment when I thought that my motoring career was going to end almost as soon as it had begun. But there is always someone behind the ominous headlight, and a trolley car is more maneuverable than an express train. The trolley ground to a stop in time, and our problem then was to get the Stoddard-Dayton out of its way. We did that by pushing, or my friends did, while I sat at the wheel and steered. And as I did—I guess it was almost by inadvertence—I tried slipping the gears into first. They went in, with some grumbling, and the engine started; my friends now, instead of pushing, had to run to catch up with me and climb in. A minute or so later, heady with my success, I tried shifting into second.

This was harder, and a certain amount of gear-clashing resulted. But I found that if I revved the motor and then let it slow down as I was shifting, I could make it—and there we were, not in high, to be sure (I didn't dare try for high gear), but still breezing along at a fairly comfortable rate of speed. The trouble was that by that time I was scared that my luck would run out on me if I stopped the car and started all over again. Though I had four or five fellows in the car whom I'd promised to take home, I didn't stop for any of them. Instead, I made my deliveries on a kind of catch-as-catch-can basis. I would drive past a boy's house—Bill Ingle's, Charlie Bowman's, Bub Schaeffer's, whoever—slow down as much as I dared, and he'd jump for it.

"So long!" we'd yell, and when he had picked himself up, he would yell back. We'd go on to the next fellow's house, and so on until I had delivered everyone. Next day, my father and I repaired the car (it was only a broken connecting link that was responsible) in the driveway to our garage.

Garages were not only rare, they were also curiously suspect. Perhaps because the whole craft was so new, automobile mechanics were regarded with a mistrustful and even somewhat hostile eye. (It occurs to me now, as I write, that I must still retain some traces of that attitude. I live most of the time in the country, and if I take my car into the local garage for repairs, I like to hang around with it, while the work is going on, so I can sort of keep track of what's going on.) In those days, everyone did all but the major repairs himself, and it was considered not only slightly sissy but also a little bit feckless to do otherwise.

Best of all, fixing, tuning, "readying" the car for a trip was something that everyone had a hand in. It was truly a function of the family; and though I can't tell whether it was by accident or by a kind of parallel functional development (which came first, the hand-churned ice-cream freezer or the cool cellarway in which it was operated?), the home architecture of the period was admirably adapted to the enterprise.

The driveway beside the house, leading back to the little garage at the rear, made an ideal spot for our car repairing. There was the outside lawn spigot handy for water for washing, and there were the steps of the back porch, perfect either as seats for the onlookers or as a place to lay out tools and spare parts. (About all one needed of the former were a long-handled screw driver, some wrenches, and— a minor but, still, important item—a few pieces of emery cloth.) There were, finally, the sun and air and the cheerful neighborhood feeling (a few back yards up the block, the Bensons were working on their Hupmobile; a few down, there was a roar as the Benedicts, experimentally, started their Oldsmobile) to give zest and a sense of common endeavor to the enterprise. And if an occasional youngster stopped by to watch, it only gave the teen-age worker, like myself, an added feeling of his own importance.

The trouble was that, once begun, the operation was quite likely to go on indefinitely. The problem, really, was to know when to stop, and in the pleasure of dismantling the engine, one was likely to forget that everything that had been taken apart would, eventually, have to be put together again. One began, ordinarily, by cleaning the spark plugs. That was where the emery cloth came into use, for the plugs were always getting fouled by the carbon residues in the burned gasoline, thus short-circuiting the spark; and once they had been unscrewed from the cylinder head, the technique was to douse them in a small can of gasoline, brush them thoroughly, and then polish them up with the emery until they were shining clean again.

Afterward, one tested them, to see how "fat" the spark was. We did this by getting out that now-vanished but useful object the crank, and turning the engine over slowly, by hand, meanwhile peering over the radiator top to see how bright and business-like-looking the little sizzle of electricity seemed as it popped in each plug in turn. Since one never knew, really, how fat the spark should be (all one knew was that there was always room for improvement), the temptation was well-nigh irresistible to go on and check over the rest of the electrical equipment.

My approach to electricity is and always has been gingerly. But I had to go through the motions—taking off the distributor cap and fiddling around with the springs and the little rotor inside (it had something to do with routing the current from one cylinder to another, but all I ever did was to blow on it, to make sure it wasn't dusty, and maybe give the "points" a wipe or two with the emery), and then checking the connections from battery to coil and from coil to distributor—and, if anyone else happened to be around, talk knowingly the while.

Next, one checked the carburetor, tightening a little screw that controlled the gasoline flow to "lean" the mixture, and then backing it off a little to be on the safe side. We did a good deal of all this empirically (if the engine ran afterward, without missing or backfiring, we considered that things were all right; if it didn't, we just tried another adjustment) and with frequent consultations of the driver's manual, which had come with the car.

The driver's manual, incidentally, instead of being the thinly veiled but totally uninformative eulogy of one's particular fluid drive, double-action brakes, and so on that it is now, was a good-sized volume, often running to sixty or seventy pages, and giving minute instructions for doing everything from adjusting the fan belt to replacing the rear axle. In those days, it had to.

Meantime, my mother would be polishing the brasswork, cleaning the windshield, brushing out the interior. Later on, if the job was a lengthy one, she might bring out a platter of sandwiches and a pitcher of iced tea, and we'd all devour them together, sitting in the lawn swing and discussing the problems at hand or the trip that was contemplated, as we did so.

It was all a great deal more fun than it may seem to have been in the telling, on a bright, sunny spring or summer Saturday, and certainly it made for a kind of companionship that seems to me to be far more valid, because it was purposeful, than the artificial sort of all-pals-together "togetherness" so much touted nowadays.

It was also extremely instructive. A few years later, I was a Naval Aviation cadet at ground school in Boston, learning to assemble and disassemble machine guns, carbines, Liberty motors, and so on. I may not have been too good on the carbines and machine guns. But on the Liberties, I was tops.

All this work of ours, ordinarily, was done in preparation for trips of some sort, and it had a certain justification, since once one was outside the city, garages were rare and dependable mechanics even more so. And my family were great picnickers. Sometimes we'd go in groups—with the Schaeffers, who had a really ancient, but still sweet-running Cadillac, or the Ostendorfs, who had a Mora—but, in any case, my mother would be busy the evening before, making lettuce-and-tomato or watercress sandwiches, cutting chicken into parts and frying them, making deviled eggs, baking cookies, filling Thermoses with iced tea and coffee; and packing all this, with various condiments, olives, pickles, and so forth, into the big picnic hamper, ready for the morning start—while my father and I, already hungering for the luncheon tomorrow, roamed the kitchen, watching, helping maybe, and occasionally sampling.

I'm sure, now, that there was a kind of friendly competitiveness involved in the feminine approach to such journeyings. If the Schaeffers, who were Pennsylvania Dutch, were joining us, we could count on one of Mrs. Schaeffer's light-as-a-feather crumb cakes; if the Ostendorfs, one of Mrs. Ostendorf's famous meringue pies. But in either case, my mother, not to be outdone, always baked one of her own specialties, either a maple walnut or a pineapple-and-vanilla layer cake. We never lacked for food on these trips of ours.

So far, I've been speaking only of Rochester. But in the period I'm concerned with—what might be called the pre-automation, or do-it-yourself era of automobiling—we lived also in Cincinnati and in Buffalo, and so our itineraries varied.

Out of Cincinnati there were lovely drives, up and down the Ohio River—up toward Point Pleasant, General Grant's birthplace, and at that time a small, quiet, white-painted, almost New England town; or down through the increasingly "southern" region toward Louisville—or, even better, across the river and into Kentucky, where the areas back of Covington were wild indeed, rough, poverty-ridden, and mountainous, and it was easy to imagine that every sidehill shanty housed a moonshiner, ready with his rifle to take a shot at us if we stopped or even lingered.

Out of Buffalo, there was a wonderful highway, brick-paved and canted at the curves like the Indianapolis Speedway—on which, in my imaginings, I was always partly, shadowily driving, every time we took the car out in that direction—leading up to Niagara Falls; and we used it a lot, chiefly taking out-of-town visitors to see the Falls, during our Buffalo sojourn.

But we seldom got there during the time we lived in Rochester, and the reasons, again, were peculiar to that era. Although Buffalo was only some sixty to seventy miles away from Rochester, there was a town, Batavia, that stood in the way; and Batavia, then, was notorious not only for its low speed limit and strict enforcement of it—as I recollect, it was a dismal ten miles per hour—but also for its fiendishly muddy roads.

Batavia, Heaven help it (and I'm sure Heaven has; from what I hear, it is now a thriving community, full of movie theaters and supermarkets, and practically all concrete), was then a stubborn roadblock in the way of progress, and, in general, our excursions were routed away from it or around it.

There were still plenty of other regions to choose from. Indeed, many of the happiest memories of my youth have to do with our trips—down to Watkins Glen and the Finger Lakes, or to Honeoye Falls; north to Lake Ontario and then east along the lake front to Sodus Point and beyond; west toward Brockport or Hamlin.

In those days, perhaps because there were few main highways, and one road was almost as good as another, we *really* wandered, and the wonderfully evocative place names of western New York State unquestionably helped to lead us on. Geneseo, Keuka, and Cattaraugus, were some of them; and, in a different genre, Warsaw, Naples and Albion, Sweden and Cuba. . . . Who wouldn't be willing to drive a few hours or so, on a pleasant Sunday, to see what Riga or West Greece looked like?

Once outside the city, though, as I've said, we were pretty much on our own. Off the main roads, gasoline was still sold mostly by the local grocery stores—a practice that still obtains in many rural regions, by the way, though now, of course they have conventional tank dispensers—and drawn gallon by gallon from a drum kept prudently outside. This left it open to the possibility of contamination; the wise motorist brought along his own funnel, with a piece of chamois to use as a strainer, and one frequently found bits of sediment in it, or maybe a few drops of rain water—deadly stuff in a carburetor—after a filling.

Punctures, blowouts, one fixed one's self. The demountable rim, which could be unbolted from the rest of the wheel and removed with the tire still on it, had come in by then, and this meant that one could carry a spare. Most people carried a couple of them, strapped on at the rear; the really smart motorist brought along one or two fresh tubes as well, stored away in the tool compartment, underneath the back seat.

The punctures still occasionally outnumbered the reinforcements, however, for one or two such mishaps per trip were considered about average. I still recall one long trip we made, to the Indian Mounds along the Scioto River east of Cincinnati, over terrible roads and, as it turned out, mostly in rain, when on the last lap home everyone in the car sat tense, not saying anything, but *pressing*—the way baseball players *press* in the dugout around the eighth and ninth innings, when a no-hit game is in the making—till we did get home, and garaged the car, and then jumped out and started congratulating one another.

"Do you realize it?" we cried. "All that way, and not a single flat tire!"

When we did run out of replacements, the only thing for it was to get out the Shaler portable vulcanizer, and make our own repairs. Who Mr. Shaler was I have no way of knowing, but to my mind his ingenious invention—a sort of small combination vise and vulcanizing oven—was the greatest single boon ever given to the venturesome motorists of that period.

To be sure, its operation was a little complicated. Having taken off the rim from the wheel, then the tire from the rim and the tube from the tire, one had next to find the leak itself. This was almost invariably caused by a horseshoe or other kind of nail (in those days, somehow, the back-country roads seemed to be strewn with them), and one located its point of entry by pumping up the spent tube—by hand, of course—till one heard the hiss of escaping air and could track down the source of it. Then one scraped the rubber around the spot with a piece of glass or some sandpaper, squeezed some goo from a tube of rubber cement out over the area, cut a patch to fit from a sheet of raw rubber supplied for that purpose, and pressed it on, clamped the section being worked on into the vise, touched a match ("Fred!" my mother would cry to my father. "Be careful now!") to a tiny canister of gasoline set beneath it, and in two or three minutes it was done, the tube not only patched, but vulcanized.

That is, if you hadn't let it "cook" too long, in which case the rubber would be cracked and weakened—or too little, when the whole patch would eventually work itself loose and peel off. In either case, though, it would last until you got home.

The tire was pumped up afterward—again, by hand—

and here the danger was that the valve, screwed out, of course, to deflate the tube, and screwed in again to inflate it, would turn out now, somehow, to be leaky. I don't know why they leaked, but they did, and rather sneakily, too, always waiting until you had the tire pumped up and were detaching the pump before, again by a fatal hissing of air, announcing their defection.

In that event, the only thing to do was to put in a new valve and start pumping again. Our tires, I remember, took two hundred and fifty pumps to come up to pressure.

Yet, for all that, we managed to take such mishaps in stride. One reason, I think, was that motoring was still more or less an outdoor sport, as skiing is nowadays, and a certain amount of hardship was expected in connection with it. Schedules were not so tight, either, which made a difference. Cars were used not so much to *get* somewhere, and, damn it, on time, too, as just to be *going* somewhere— and if not *there* precisely, well, maybe, somewhere else.

And the countryside was wide, empty, and inviting; if a breakdown occurred, the ladies piled out to sit in the shade on the grass by the roadside, and offer encouragement, while the men shucked their jackets and started repairing. If there was a brook or some other likely spot nearby, we would probably picnic right there.

Motoring was a sport in other ways, too, and a lively one, as I look back on it. Maybe just because he didn't do much of the driving—he early discovered he was far too absent-minded for that—my father was the most adventurous of us all. Underneath his Yankee restraint there was a streak almost of recklessness, and it was always he, on the one hand, who suggested turning off the main road onto a byway, and then from that onto a woods road, snaking off, possibly, up a mountain ("But it looks interesting, doesn't it?" he would reply to my mother's objections); and it was he—vicariously but always wholeheartedly—who got us into the impromptu but desperate "brushes" that were common then on the highways.

These, I imagine, were translations into the motor age of similar encounters in the days of sulkies and blooded horses; in any case, the sounding of one's horn (a Klaxon, of course) and a gesture toward passing the car ahead was almost certain to be interpreted as a challenge.

It did not matter in the least that you might be hurrying to keep an appointment while the man ahead of you had been merely loafing along, enjoying the scenery. On the instant, his pride, not only in his prowess as a driver but also in the performance of his car, was called into question. He would glance back briefly, disdainfully, and then bend his head down, settling at the wheel, stepping on the accelerator. Before you knew it, you were either involved in a road race or, craven, resigned yourself to following your leader at his own triumphant pace.

My father never invited such races, and if a man wanted to pass us, he was always—well, almost always—willing to let him pass. But if the man in front of us speeded up, that was different, and though I was naturally far more cautious than he, he somehow managed to infect me. I still remember one Sunday morning when we went racing pell-mell down the winding hill roads leading into Canandaigua, on the wrong side of the road and side by side with a competitive Oldsmobile—myself shrunken with fear at our speed but by that time still more scared of slowing down—until, fortunately, just short of the town's main street, my adversary "chickened" and slacked off, and we went ahead in, to me, a sort of terrified triumph.

The rear seat of the car containing my mother and an

aunt who was visiting us at the time, had been in an uproar throughout. But my father had never turned a hair.

"Well, I guess we taught that man something about the courtesies of the road," he said complacently, as we whizzed past the startled congregation of a church just letting out, and then on into the center of the town.

 eight

To come back to the old cars themselves, and in particular to our Stoddard-Dayton, it was, in addition to its racy appearance, something of a rarity, too—since, as the name implies, it was manufactured in Dayton, Ohio, and the make was not common in western New York State. In its own way, it was almost as exotic as a Sunbeam or a Citröen on the streets of New York today, and attracted something of the same attention. People, seeing it at the curb, used often to ask what make it was—a circumstance, of course, that in no way displeased me, or, for the matter of that, my father.

But it occurs to me that all this, in view of present conditions, may require a word of explanation. Even at that time (to remove any too great suggestion of antediluvianism, it was around 1914), there was a sizable number of cars that were sold nationally. I can think, offhand, of the Ford, Reo, Hupmobile, Cadillac, Dodge, Buick, Oldsmobile, and, among the most expensive machines, the Lozier, Peerless, Winton, and Pierce-Arrow. There were, though, a great many others that were still pretty much local products, built in small plants by local designers, and sold more or

less exclusively in the region where they were manufactured.

I had run into this fact accidentally, a few years earlier,
when we had been living in Springfield, Massachusetts. The
cars one saw there, in addition to the national brands, were
the Stevens-Duryea (another of the really "fine" cars, made
in Chicopee Falls, a few miles outside the city) and the
Atlas, a short-lived and now almost-forgotten machine
which was made in a little shop so close to our own home
that the cars were test-driven around our neighborhood;
I used to see, and envy, the drivers, sitting on rough board
seats mounted on the bare chassis, putting the new cars
through their paces. The Stanley Steamer, another Massa-
chusetts-made car, was also popular there, as were also the
Pope-Hartford and the Locomobile, which, as I recall, was
manufactured in Bridgeport, Connecticut.

The Pope Motor Car Company, in what now seems a
primitive gesture toward chain-store operation, had another factory in Toledo, Ohio—where they made, of
course, the Pope-Toledo—and they also had another car,
an electric, which was called the Pope-Waverly. Other
Midwestern cars were the Moline-Knight and the Stearns-
Knight, the Cole, the Studebaker, the Hudson, the Apper-
son "Jack-Rabbit," the Rambler, and the Maxwell. I am
sure there were hundreds of others produced still farther
west—say, in California—that were never even seen in our
part of the country.

And there *were* hundreds of others. One night, a few
years ago, I sat up with a couple of advertising men from
Detroit, and for no particular reason we began trying to see
how many names of old motorcars we could think of.
They came up with the most, being in the business. But I
supplied quite a few, and in the end we had listed well over

a hundred. Later, looking the matter up, I discovered we hadn't even scratched the surface.

According to a list compiled by the Encyclopedia Americana, there were over twenty-five hundred different makes of motorcars manufactured at one time or another, in this country. They varied from the most wildly experimental to the astonishingly foresighted—or, to give a few examples, from a contraption called the "Octomobile," which had two sets of four wheels each, front and rear, like a railway carriage (it was supposed to be easier riding), to the Cole, which I've just mentioned, and which had the first automatic gearshift, and the Mora, which had the first coil-spring suspension.

Now—or at last count, anyway—there are twelve, put out by only four manufacturers, and to me it's a sad commentary on the course of free enterprise.

To come back to Rochester and our Stoddard-Dayton: Rochester, too, had its share of local favorites, though ours was not among them. Rochester was the home of, among others, the Cunningham, a conservative, substantial car (the firm, typically, continued to manufacture high-class hearses long after its pleasure-car market had vanished), and the Selden. The latter was made by a man named George S. Selden, an astute patent lawyer who achieved a curious fame by securing a patent on the whole concept of the gasoline engine well before he had even built one (the real early inventors, men like Henry Ford, Alexander Winton, Elwood Haynes, and the Duryea brothers, just built their engines and cars and never thought of patenting them), and succeeded for years in collecting royalties from all the other less foresighted manufacturers until Ford, stubbornly, resisted, and stopped him.

The Franklin, made in nearby Syracuse, was common,

too (it had an air-cooled engine, as the Volkswagen has now, and, for reasons that escape me at the moment, boasted in its advertising of a tubular front axle and a laminated-wood chassis-frame), and so was the Pierce-Arrow, manufactured in Buffalo and for a long time the official White House vehicle. Possibly because Rochester was so very flat (the only eminence I can recall was Cobb's Hill, out by the reservoir, where we used to go bobsledding, winters), the low-powered Rauch & Lang Electrics were popular, too.

The electrics had quite a vogue for a while, by the way, as did also the steam-powered automobiles, and there are still a few venerable enthusiasts who contend that the Stanley Steamer was one of the finest motorcars ever built anywhere. Designed by the two Stanley brothers, of Newton, Massachusetts, and built with almost watchlike precision (during most of the firm's life, they produced less than a thousand cars a year), it was, for its time, almost unbelievably fast and powerful.

One of them, anyway, is credited with a cool 127.6 miles per hour, registered in a time trial on Ormond Beach, Florida, as far back as 1906, and they were so famous for their ability to chug their way up any grade on which their tires could find traction that they were considered *hors concours* and barred from most hill-climbing competitions.

But the electrics went under the disadvantage of having to be plugged into an electric outlet at fairly frequent intervals to be recharged—often, naturally, something of a problem when on the road—while the steamers suffered two handicaps: one being that it required about a half hour or so to fire up the boiler (it was heated by an alcohol burner), and, two, a fairly widespread suspicion that they might at any moment explode. This, the steamer people insisted, was a canard circulated by the gasoline-engine interests; and it certainly seems to have had little foundation, for as far as I ever heard none of the steam cars ever did blow up—and there were, for a while, a number of other makes besides the original Stanley, including the White, the Doble, and so on.

For that matter, the steam people may have done their share of propagandizing, too—as witnessed by the fact that there were many people, my own grandmother among them, who were reluctant to ride in cars like the Model T Ford, which had the gas tank placed right under the driver's seat, on the ground that *it* might go up, too, taking driver and passengers with it. In the end, anyway, the gasoline motor won out.

The electrics, however, though slow, were extremely simple of operation. There was only one pedal, the brake, and you moved a handle to control the speed. You steered, too, by a handle bar, this one horizontal, and the two passengers rode in an odd clover-leaf fashion, one beside the driver and the other in the corner diagonally opposite, with his back to the windshield. But they were beautifully constructed, with a closed-in, glassed-in body more or less like an old-fashioned brougham in styling, and full of padded upholstery, fine wood trim, flower vases, and so on; and for all these reasons, in addition to the crowning one that they required no cranking, they were regarded as preeminently the proper car for a lady.

My mother, who, as I've said, was something of a feminist, thought differently, and she learned to drive just about as soon as my father and I did. But she was a rarity, and, in general, the complexities of the gasoline engine were considered to be beyond the grasp of the feminine mind. In those days, if a woman wanted to go marketing, she hopped into the electric instead of, as now, into the station wagon;

and the two-car garage, of a family prosperous enough to afford one, ordinarily contained a gasoline-powered car on the master's side and an electric on the other.

At that time, though, and for a good many years thereafter, our little Stoddard-Dayton satisfied all our needs, and it was a good car throughout, fast, handy, and reliable. I'd like to place a special emphasis on that last word, "reliable." I realize that I may have been picturing early motoring, so far, as an almost continuous series of breakdowns, blowouts, and similar mishaps. But to leave it at that would be to distort the picture. We drove hundreds of trouble-free miles for every one where we had a puncture; and though it's true that such bothersome things did occur—and with far greater frequency than they now do—they occurred, and in a way that seems somehow mysterious to me now, *conveniently*.

Even accidents had the same casual, innocent flavor, and in my view this had something to do with the simple sturdiness of the cars' construction itself. In my experience, the Ford Model T was the last to have this friendly, companionable quality.

I had most to do with these some years later, in the course of a summer spent at the artists' colony at Woodstock, New York, and the Ford there was practically universal. (You bought one, secondhand, at Longyear's or Allen's garage for fifty dollars at the beginning of summer and sold it back in the fall for twenty-five, repeating the process the following year.) The time was the height of the prohibition era, and the wrecks that resulted as people drove home from Saturday-night cider or applejack parties, up or down the winding Catskill hill roads, were sensational.

Fords rammed into trees or into embankments, slipped

off culverts or into ditches, but the damage to the occupants and even to the cars was always minimal. One Sunday
morning, for instance, two village ladies, heading for
church, came upon a Ford overturned by the side of the
road and saw its occupants, motionless and apparently
dead, lying on the grass nearby. The ladies hurried into the
village, telephoned the hospital at Kingston, and walked
back to the scene—to find it deserted. The party-goers had
simply come to, heaved the Ford back onto its wheels
again, and, no doubt unsteadily, driven off home.

Woodstock people, though, may have been hardier than
most, and certainly they were heavier drinkers. Liquor
played no part in my youthful adventures, but there was
the same companionable feeling about a car in a time of
trouble.

We had a Paige, for instance (another now-forgotten
make), that always broke down, if it was *going* to break
down, right in front of our house—except when once, in
Frankfort, Kentucky, its rear axle gave way in front of the
very hotel we'd planned to stop at for the night. This truly
was a major accident, and one outcome of it was that we
spent two or three not unenjoyable days in Frankfort,
while the local garageman sent away for the necessary parts
to make the repairs. But if it had happened even a few minutes earlier, as we were racing, late, down the steep, winding roads leading into the city, we should almost certainly
all have been killed.

In those days, most mishaps lacked even such overtones
of possible disaster, and many times they even gave an
extra fillip of excitement to what would otherwise have
been a humdrum trip.

Once, a failure of our lighting system gave me what I
still recall as a glimpse of a peculiarly charming rustic para-

dise. This was still in our Stoddard-Dayton days, and our headlights were lit by acetylene gas—Prest-O-Lite, it was called—carried under pressure in a copper tank on the running board and piped to the big brass lamps out front. And they hadn't actually failed; the tank had simply run out, as we'd discovered, driving a little later than usual, the night before.

I was on my way to New Haven to register for college entrance, and we had made a family trip of it; we were in Middletown, Connecticut, next morning when we inquired about getting a fresh tank, filled with gas, to replace our empty one.

There was some complication here whose details I can't recall now, for, normally, the procedure would have been to replace the tank at a garage. This time, though, we were directed to a place just outside town where the gas was made and the actual filling of the tanks was done. Shortly afterward, where the road ran alongside a reach of the broad, bland, smoothly flowing Connecticut River, we drew up at the plant itself.

I realize now it couldn't have been as idyllic as I recall it, but at the moment I had my own special reasons for seeing it so. I was entering college; and that, though a large and in some ways a fearsome step forward in my career, was only incidental to a larger purpose of mine. I wanted to be a poet, and since it had been well brought home to me, by apparently wholly credible testimony, that poets didn't make any money to speak of, I spent a good deal of my time trying to think of jobs or occupations that would provide me with a living—bare, or, at the best, nearly bare; half-clothed with the ordinary comforts, as it were—while I puttered away at my poems.

Something sedentary was what was needed, and also

something that required as little effort and responsibility as possible. I had thought, as I suppose every youngster has thought, of being a lighthouse tender. But that seemed a little too remote. And the idea of being a crossing-tender on the railroad still appealed to me, too, till I learned that such jobs were reserved for old railroaders, too superannuated for other duties. I had even toyed, occasionally, with the idea of a life of crime, or, if not that exactly, of pulling a big job—twenty, thirty, or forty thousand dollars or so; one read about them constantly in the newspapers—and then retiring to some distant mountain cabin, to use the money to finance whole years and years of uninterrupted writing. But I didn't know how to get *started* on a life of crime, holding up banks and whatnot, and, besides, I was by nature a little cautious.

Now, here before me was what seemed to be the perfect solution, and I can only describe it as I recall it. A man, lying back in a lawn chair, reading a book; behind him, a neat little house, obviously his dwelling; at one side, a large shed, or barn, where the gas was produced; and, in front of that, a long series of low wooden racks, in which the tanks being refilled were installed. Beyond all that, the broad Connecticut River, flowing placidly.

The man, small, dark-haired, neat, and quiet-mannered, was pleasantness itself. I believe we had our tank filled on the spot, instead of taking a replacement; in any case, we were there for a little time, enough for him to show us around the place, including the shed that served as his acetylene-gas factory, if so it may be called.

I don't remember much of that, except for an impression of storage tanks, vats, and a good deal of piping. But I learned later, in chemistry course, that the gas is a natural product of the action of water on calcium carbide, and it was obvious even then that all the man had to do was to mix these substances in their proper proportions, check a gauge or two maybe, occasionally, for pressures and such-like, and, of course, unhitch the filled tanks and replace them with empties.

All the rest of his time he had to himself, and I looked at him with envy. He gardened, he said (he did have some beautiful roses), and he read a good deal, which may have been one reason he and my father hit it off so well together, for my father was also a great reader. But if I'd been in the man's place, of course, I'd have written, and I could think of no better place than this calm, shady, river-lapped haven to do it in.

College, I decided, would be all right and probably fun, but as a preparation for a career it would certainly be useless, for from now on my mind was made up and I knew what I was going to do. As soon as I graduated, I was going to get myself a Prest-O-Lite agency like this one, and settle down to a pleasantly bucolic, almost effortless literary existence. I never did, though—and, anyway, by the time I got out of college, electric lighting had replaced gas in just about all the cars made.

 nine

I have a host of other random recollections about the early automobiles and me. Though the fact may be almost forgotten now, we *named* our cars in the old days, for they were not then the bleak, interchangeable units from an endless assembly line they are now; instead, they had—or they seemed to us to have—the proud, individual character of yachts, and it was in that sense that we named them. Lately, I've been casting about in my own mind, and probing those of such friends as I can get at, to resurrect a few examples of early nomenclature.

Odd though some of them may seem, I prefer them to the examples of ready-made nomenclature, often chromium-inscribed on the fender or trunk lid—"Star-Flite," "Jet-Flite," "Impala," and so on—that the automobile manufacturers now pin on their products.

Our Stoddard-Dayton, because of its color, was always called "Brownie," and the Paige that came after it—owing, I think, to some defect in its headlights—was christened "Blinky." The Chrysler that followed *it* marked, obviously, the change from the sentimental to the purely practical era, for, as far as I can recall, we had no name for it at all.

To give you an idea of the extent to which sentiment entered in, a friend of mine, prodded by me in the course of these researches, has suddenly recalled that when his family sold their first car—an Overland, named, fairly allusively, "The Scout"—and, the deal consummated, the new owner was driving it away, my friend's mother, standing on their front porch, watching, abruptly burst into tears.

"I hope he takes good care of it!" she wailed, with all the poignance that accompanies a parting with a good friend or servitor after years of faithful companionship. We had something of the same feeling after we'd traded our Paige for the Chrysler, for the older car was bought soon afterward by a junkman, who cut off the after part of the body and converted it, rather ramshackledly, into a truck. We used to hang our heads guiltily whenever we saw our old friend, thus mutilated, going by.

Our friends the Schaeffers' old Cadillac was called, affectionately, "The Ark," and another family we knew had a Rambler they nicknamed, I suppose with some vague reference to vagabondage, "Dusty." Another fellow I knew recalls that *his* family's car was called, more poetically, "Hot Spur," while another confesses shyly that their first car, a Franklin, was christened "Daisy." This really does seem to be a pretty long reach in search of allusiveness— but, as I said at first, if you think of a car in the same context as a yacht, or even a family cruiser, it becomes a good deal less startling. After all, no one laughs at even a sixteen-footer named "Rosabelle," "Princess," or "Wanderer III."

So far, I notice, I seem to have described most of our excursions as occurring in sunny weather, and I suppose on the theory that one tends to remember the pleasant things rather than the unpleasant, this is only natural. We did run into rain, though, on occasion, and my most vivid memories about that have to do with the moments before the downpour came, when a ritual called "beating the storm" was enacted by every motorist worthy of the name.

This, of course, is unknown in these modern days of cars that are either totally enclosed or have tops, motor-operated, which go up at the touch of a button. The early tops, however, were the one feature of the old motorcars that I remember with distaste. Big, clumsy, broad-beamed affairs, with their heavy wooden ribs and billowing canvas, they were a direct descendant of the bowed top of the prairie schooner, which they much resembled, and they were as difficult to get up as they were to put down and stow away again. Is it any wonder that, when a storm loomed suddenly, the slow, peaceful traffic along the highway would be turned into a mad scramble, as everyone stepped on the gas and did his damnest to get away from it?

I should add, too, that my own excursions weren't all family affairs, either. I hope I offend no Rochesterian, of either my own or other generations, by saying that Rochester was a big country town in what I may be allowed to call the "teen-age years" of the present century. So it was, though, or so I see it, but it was so in the pleasantest sense imaginable—the sense, to be explicit, that its streets were broad, shady, and uncrowded, the houses lining them comfortable and well-appointed, set in ample grounds, and the life itself easy, confident, and unhurried.

To complete the picture, I must add that the Rochester girls, in keeping with the town's general atmosphere, were almost without exception healthy, cheerful, fresh-skinned, and, frequently, very pretty. And I was just in my middle teens at the time, at the age when a boy is beginning to realize, even if a little reluctantly, that girls have a place in the world, too, along with tennis, boxing, baseball, and such other masculine employments—that even, mysteriously, there is a peculiar, indescribable pleasure to be found in just teaching a girl how, say, to hold a tennis racket in one of those slim, soft, unmuscular hands, and how to swing it.

And the very easygoingness and the semirusticity of the life of Rochester were a help in this development. Winters, there was skating on Kondolf's Pond or one of the many park lakes (the boy kneeling gallantly to put on the girl's skates for her, with, usually, a bonfire roaring on the bank nearby) or bobsledding on Cobb's Hill—and always hot chocolate and cookies waiting later at someone's family's home, set out in the big basement playroom, Rochester's precocious version of what later acquired the sorry name of "rumpus room."

There were basketball games and school dances, hay rides on the big farm sledges that were still available; and, quite frequently, little impromptu dances at homes, where the girls would make fudge or Welsh rarebit, thus displaying their talents for domesticity.

In the summertime, whenever one fellow or another could borrow his family's car, there were outings—swimming parties out at someone's cottage on Lake Ontario or at camps in the Finger Lakes region—and here again the girls had a chance to show their cooking skills, for these usually included a picnic, but a more impromptu one than the adult variety.

This, perhaps, was because we were never quite sure (parents are so unaccountable) until the last minute if the car would really be available; at any rate, what we did was to bring our supplies along raw, in a manner of speaking, and prepare them on the spot.

Best of all, in my recollection, was a dish, or concoction, called the "bacon bat." I don't know if it was peculiar to Rochester or was common elsewhere. But, in any case, all you need is a few husky boys to gather wood for an open fire and get it going; some pretty girls, with makeshift aprons over their dresses and their faces flushed with the heat of the flames; a big frying pan, and some bread, eggs, bacon, and tomatoes.

After that, the procedure is simple. You just fry the bacon in the pan, scramble the eggs in the bacon fat, spread these out, with some thick tomato slices, between large hunks of bread—and there you are, the bacon bat. You eat the sandwiches standing, of course, and preferably over the fire itself, for drippings and other debris are prodigious. But, given the right circumstances, I can think of nothing else more delicious.

Afterward, we would sit around the fire for a while, watching the dying embers. Then, bundled cozily together in the open car, we would drive home, singing; and, to my mind, an open touring car, top down on a summer night, with the breeze rippling in around the windshield, and the trees rustling transitorily in the welcoming way they have, their leaves set in motion by the very rush of your passage, is still about as pleasant a means of transportation as anyone could ask for.

"Moonlight Bay" we'd sing, certainly, for it was particularly appropriate with the lake water stretching off, rippling, and, by now, possibly, even moonlit, beside us; and we all loved the wonderfully wistful effect one got when the boys, in their deeper voices, echoed the end of each line after the girls had sung it: "We were sailing along

(*We were sailing along*) on Moonlight Bay (*On Moonlight Bay*), I could hear the voices ringing. . . ."

And then also there were others, like "Sympathy" ("I need sy-*im*-pathy"), "Sayonara" ("Sweet Good-by"), and "On the Banks of the Saskatchewah" (from a play called *The Pink Lady*, starring an actress named Hazel Dawn, whom I had fallen in love with as soon as I saw her, on the stage of the Seneca Theatre). If we felt especially ambitious, we might try a few rounds: "There is a boat/Hails to the ferry," or "Big Tom is cast," or, of course, the perennial favorite, "Row, row, row your boat/Gently down the stream/Merrily, merrily, merrily, merrily/Life is but a dream."

There might have been a certain amount of hand-holding, accompanied by flashing sidelong glances, and even a discreet bit of cuddling, earlier. But a touring car makes for camaraderie rather than for romance, and a cool night breeze makes for drowsiness; if the trip was at all long, even the songs, eventually, would die. Half asleep, if not actually wholly so—all, that is, except the driver—we'd arrive home at last.

I'd learned about girls in another way, too, by means of the motorcar. I don't know if anyone else remembers the "jitney bus" era any more. I'm not even sure how localized the phenomenon was, and, hence, if it was confined to the general region of western New York State or if it spread elsewhere. All I know is that some time around 1915 or 1916, in Rochester, private cars operating like miniature buses, in competition with the trolleys, began appearing on the streets.

They lined up along the curb at the principal intersections downtown—State and Main, Main and Genesee Avenue, and so on—each with a little hand-lettered sign on the windshield stating the route it followed; the charge was a "jitney," a nickel, the same as the trolleys, and, until the novelty wore off—and until the streetcar company, after some hasty lobbying, got laws passed regarding licensing, insurance requirements, route schedules, and so on: all, till then, disregarded in those free and easy times—they were literally everywhere.

At the start, the drivers were men, but when the summer vacation came on, all the boys who could wangle the family car even part of the time got in on it as well. I was one. I don't recall how my father got to and from his office downtown, unless he rode the jitneys, too, and it must have been an inconvenience all round. But I suppose my parents figured it was good for me, since it showed enterprise, and for a couple of weeks or so, or until disillusionment set in, I drove our car as a jitney bus on the Lake Avenue line.

I had chosen Lake Avenue partly because it passed fairly near our house and was a well-traveled thoroughfare besides. But it was a handsome street, too, broad and, once one got outside the center of the city, lined with large, substantial houses. In much the same way that I suppose a man opening a stationery store takes pride in the fact that it's in a good neighborhood rather than a poor one, I took a slightly snobbish pleasure in the feeling that, if I was in business at all, it was with the best kind of people.

And I was in business, make no mistake about it. To be sure, a number of my passengers were people I knew, or my family did, and I felt at first a certain embarrassment in taking money from them. But they, as adults, laughed that aside, and I soon learned to do so, too. And I suppose there should have been a certain tedium in driving the same route over and over—down Lake Avenue to State Street and on to the intersection at Main; turn to join the line at the curb and wait there till I had my quota of passengers, and then up State to Lake and out again.

I didn't feel it, though. I was out in the world, on my own at last, and I can still see myself, and—in that odd sort of double vision that one gets with remembering—*be* myself, too, driving back and forth, back and forth, as gravely serious about my business responsibilities as only a boy of seventeen or so can be, and at the same time intensely curious, watching what went on about me.

As a matter of fact, I had very few signal adventures. There were the brushes with the trolley-car motormen, who, of course, hated us, and who, if they saw some possible passenger waiting at a corner ahead, would put on full speed in an effort to get there ahead of us. But an automobile, even then, had a quicker pickup than a trolley, and we usually got there first; even if we didn't, half the time the customer would wait for the jitney. Just riding in an automobile in those days, for a good many people, was still something of an adventure—as a plane trip now is, as compared to one on an express train. And my choice of the Lake Avenue route turned out to be a fortunate one, for it ran out to the big Eastman Kodak plant, in a parklike area of its own on the outskirts of town, and there, of course, at closing time, there were hundreds of workers looking for transportation.

I was beginning to think I had fallen on a bonanza when one day, at the plant, a remarkably pretty girl hopped into the seat beside me. (The front seat, in a jitney bus, was comparable in its attractiveness to the seat behind the motorman in an open trolley.) She was dark-haired, dark-eyed, plump, high-colored; and, pretty as she undeniably was, she was also a little frightening, for she was at least a couple of years older than I was—an intimidating thing for a fellow of seventeen—and obviously much more experienced. And instead of wrapping herself in the stiff, suspicious silence I'd already got used to in most of my other feminine passengers, she was almost alarmingly approachable. Yet for all that, I soon found myself getting along wonderfully well with her.

She was demure at first, of course, but even then there was a hint that the demureness was only external, a barrier that could easily be broken through, and when I tried out my "line" on her (as I recall, and I don't much like to, it was a mixture of jokes that were meant to be faintly risqué, mannish talk about tennis and other sports I engaged in, and dark hints about petting parties I'd been out on; and it went over pretty well with girls of my own age), she melted considerably. By the time we reached the street corner where she got off, it had somehow come to be understood that she'd ride with me regularly from then on.

I believe she paid her fare the first couple of times, though I was probably too entranced to notice. If so, it wasn't more than a few days later that it turned out she'd forgotten her purse, somehow, and was nickel-less.

"That's all right," I assured her gallantly.

"Do you mean it?" she asked. I said, sure, and from then on there was no more nonsense about paying. Clearly, she had—mistakenly, of course—taken my waiving the fare that one day to mean that I was willing to forego it forever, and I was in no state to correct her. I didn't much mind, either.

I always had three or four paying passengers in the back seat to give me some sense of profit. Besides, I felt I was beginning to make headway with her, though I was a little uncertain in what direction. I never tried to make a date with her. I had a feeling she'd be far too worldly for me, for one thing; for another, she was a factory girl, and in the middle-class morality of those times, that automatically made her a little bit suspect.

Factory girls were considered to be "wild," and I was afraid that if I got too involved with her, I might "get beyond my depth," in some way. Who knows, I might even have to marry her! Yet I was still fascinated with her, and I would gladly have ferried her home from work all summer, for free, if she hadn't started ringing her friends in on me.

Only a day or so later, she turned up with another girl. The new one was not so pretty, either, but since they got off together I could hardly collect the fare from one and not from the other. And the next day—having thus felt the ground out, I suppose—she appeared with a whole clutch of them; and when *they* got off, again all together, it turned out that none of them expected to pay, either. To be sure, one did start to reach for her purse, but my girl put a stop to that immediately.

"Oh, he doesn't let *us* pay!" she cried. "Do you, babe?" I grinned weakly, I guess, and with that they all ran off up the street. I suppose I might even have let that pass, I was so bemused, if a couple of them, a few steps away, hadn't laughed. And I was at that age when a boy is peculiarly sensitive to the sound of girls laughing, mysteriously, anywhere around him.

For all I know, they may have been laughing at something utterly unrelated to me, though I doubt it. But in my mind that laugh struck home, and in a flash I saw myself as I was sure they must see me—a poor, callow, young fool, boastful with nothing to boast of (I remembered I'd been telling them, in great detail, only a few minutes before, how I'd almost won the West High School tennis championship that spring), and a snobbish little twerp, too, for the matter of that, though I don't think the full realization of that came until later—now left grinning stupidly in my father's car, while they made a mock of me.

I had been in a slightly similar mess before, when things had gotten out of hand with a woman, only that time the woman had been my mother. She and I were on a streetcar, riding home from some shopping trip downtown, and on boarding it I had absent-mindedly slid into the favored seat by the window, leaving her to take the one on the aisle. I had hardly got settled there before I realized I had put myself in a position no true gentleman should ever be found in—since a gentleman, unfailingly, always saw his lady seated, and in the most comfortable condition, before himself sitting down.

I solved that problem by simply withdrawing from it. Or, rather, I withdrew, for the duration of the journey, from my mother. In a sense, I dematerialized her. I pretended she just wasn't there, or if she was, I wasn't acquainted with her, and I spent the rest of the trip, and it was a fairly long one, staring fixedly out the window.

The only trouble was, I had no way of conveying this new attitude of mine to my mother, and it puzzled her. We'd been talking fairly animatedly before, and this sudden uncommunicativeness on my part confused her completely. "Are you all right? Is anything the matter?" I remember her asking once, and I muttered, from the side of my mouth. "Yes. Yes. I'm all right. Just don't feel like talking, that's all." Finally, bewildered but compliant, she, too, lapsed into silence.

I solved my problem with the Kodak girls in a somewhat similar fashion—by just withdrawing from them, and from jitney-bus driving, entirely. My parents, I remember, were disappointed to see my first business venture ending so abruptly; and since again I couldn't explain the true situation, I'm afraid they took it as just another example of that footlessness I was always being accused of. But I couldn't help it, under the circumstances. I was darned if I was going to be taken in by those girls again—not if I could help it!

 ten

Clarence Simmons & Son is the name of the firm that de-
livers fuel oil to me at my place in the country, and Chauncy
French & Son run our local garage. Often, as I make out the
checks for their monthly bills, I find myself thinking re-
gretfully of the one circumstance in which I disappointed
my father badly. As I've already said, he was a mechanical
engineer who developed into a designer of special machinery, and since he was a sentimentalist, with a strong
background of Yankee traditionalism and continuity to
boot, it was his dearest desire, his wish of wishes, to see me
follow in the same line, to the end that his company's title
"Frederick Coates, Machine Design" be augmented by the
magic term "& Son," and a new engineering dynasty be
born.

I failed him in that, for my tastes ran far too determinedly
in another direction, but I had to come within about three
thousandths of an inch of losing my right forefinger to do it.
In another sense, though, my father defeated himself, for
he tried too hard, and that in itself was enough to lick him.
There is probably no more difficult, delicate, and thank-
less task a parent can undertake than an attempt to guide,

117

lure, or inveigle a child into a career of his (the parent's) choosing. He can't pull him, he can't push him; in either case, the recalcitrant youngster's heels dig in; all the wariness and that sense of being *different* that marks even the happiest relationship between generations—and the feeling of wanting to develop the differences in one's own way —come into play, to the parent's and in a sense also the child's frustration.

Guile, I suppose, is required if the parent is to succeed, and my father was about as free from guile as any man I have ever known. Doomed to failure or not, though, Lord knows he tried—in that gentle, unassertive way that was part of his nature. As I can see now, indeed, the campaign got under way—I'm sure unconsciously on his part, however—away back in my early childhood, for one of the first toys I had that I can remember clearly was a miniature stationary steam engine that he gave me for my sixth or seventh birthday.

It was a handsome little thing, with a brass-bound boiler, brass-ornamented piston, cylinder, flywheel, and other parts, and a tall black smokestack to top it off. It was mounted on a small flat base about two feet square and floored with a green-and-white-checked linoleum to simulate tile, and, best of all, it worked! All you had to do was to light the wick of a little tin container, filled with alcohol, in the firebox under the boiler, and, by virtue of James Watt's ancient magic, the water in the boiler turned gradually to steam, and the steam, confined, to power: before you knew it, the cylinder was hissing and spouting, the piston chugging busily back and forth, and the big flywheel turning steadily and majestically. In the year or two following, I was given a number of subsidiary toy machines— a little lathe and an equally tiny circular saw, both exquisitely made, are the ones I remember—which could be made to run by a belt from the engine's flywheel.

I was impressed, I must confess. But in this case, as in other later attempts, my father was defeated by his own eagerness. The trouble here was that I was just too young for so complicated a plaything. It was my mother who decided that. Though normally adventurous enough, she still had a few of the conventional "ladylike" fears of her period, among them snakes, bats, mice, and explosives, and she flatly refused to allow me to tinker, alone, with that baleful alcohol lamp and boiler. In the end, it was my father who "played," with rather forced enthusiasm, with the engine and the rest of the outfit, while I looked on, more and more uninterested. The whole apparatus was discarded, as I recall, a few years later.

So it went. I got Meccano sets when I wanted the *Oxford Book of English Verse;* a slide rule when I was far too young to attempt to use it, much less understand its workings. His greatest mistake, though, came one summer in Rochester, when he took me on to work through the summer as a sort of apprentice-helper in his shop.

I was in high school by then, and the shop occupied a floor in a big, gaunt, yellow-brick loft building, filled with similar small factories and other enterprises, on North Main Street. I can still remember the look and sounds of it: the whir and slap of the belts running down from the pulleys on the long overhead power shafts to the aisled rows of machines lined up underneath; the dusty windows and the electric lights, always on, shining bleakly down from their cone-shaped reflectors on the gleaming steel, channeled surface of a lathe bed, the blunt shuttling head of a shaper, or the slithery-with-oil, flat face of a drill-press table (the whole giving a curiously dramatic sense of alternating brilliance and dimness); the thick-timbered, greasy surface of the big workbenches beyond; and the men, moving about here and there or working intent at their jobs—or, alternately and inexplicably to me, suddenly singing, joking, or skylarking.

My father had about a dozen men on the payroll, all strangers to me, of course, and armed, too, with the added strangeness that adulthood holds for a boy in his teens; to them, I was the boss's son and so from the start a little suspect, and, all in all, it was some time before I even got them sorted out in my mind. Every skilled trade, I've since learned, has its hierarchy, but the mechanic's, being more skilled than most, has a correspondingly more fixed and inflexible one. At the top is the toolmaster, represented in our shop by a lean, elderly Yankee named Jess Griswold, who was also the foreman, and at the bottom is the apprentice-helper, in this case, me. In between are the various machine operators, with the lathe hand at the head of these, since it takes a fairly high degree of skill, judgment, and experience to "true up" a piece of metal in the turret of a lathe and turn it down to exact dimensions; and the list came full circle when I was assigned to be Mr. Griswold's helper.

I didn't last long at this, and not much longer anywhere else in the shop, for that matter. But I did last long enough to get at least an inkling of what a complex little world, at once ingrown, compact, and yet curiously varied, a small shop can be.

It has its cliques and its rivalries and its abrupt flare-ups of bitter bad temper, but if it's a well-run place, it has a kind of cool, carefree *esprit de corps* that overrides them. Perhaps oddest of all, it has daily, small, definite emotional cycles, and it is a foolish foreman indeed who interferes too much with them. Possibly because so much of the work is done to extremely close tolerance and hence requires the strictest attention; maybe, too, because the muscular demands, though often considerable, must be carefully measured (one turns up the wrench or one shifts the block just enough, not too much, not too little), there comes almost inevitably a moment in the day when the strains and the tensions on everyone reach a common peak, and the only release that can be found is in a kind of simultaneous blow-off.

If the general mood is right, the littlest thing can set it off. Someone shies a paper plate, left over from lunch, down the room, and in an instant everyone is scrambling for it; two men meet in an aisle and for no reason at all—and with no ill-feeling, either—start wrestling; a piece of waste, wadded up, becomes a baseball, to be batted enthusiastically back and forth. Perhaps pleasantest of all, someone, set off by the steady drone of his machine, starts a song, and again if the mood is right, the song spreads until finally almost every man in the shop has joined in, and one sees a whole row of solemn, singing heads, spotlighted by the overhead bulbs and all nodding choirlike in time to the tune, along the ranked machines. Mr. Griswold, who was rather a cantankerous old cuss—as most toolmakers are—smiled sourly at such high jinks. But even he rarely intervened.

I learned, too, that if shops have their hierarchies, they also have what amounts to an oddly standard uniform cast of characters. In the course of my school years, I had a number of other jobs (in my youth, it was felt that a boy *should* work summers; it taught him the value of money). I worked as yardman at Eastman Kodak, in a tire plant, and as a helper in a furniture factory, among other places, and I found the same basic characters reappearing so often that it began to seem as if the whole world might be a kind of mo-

rality play after all, like Everyman, with the allegory repeated, in miniature, in the population of the various shops.

Our shop was no exception. Our Mr. Wiseman, our
scholar, and a thwarted actor no doubt, was a stoop-shoul-
dered, ruddy-faced balding man whose name I forget but
who was noted equally for the fact that he was the father of
no less than nine children and had yet found time to get an
astonishing amount of Shakespeare down by heart. There
was no fooling about it, either. He could, and frequently
did, recite all Hamlet's soliloquies, the balcony scene from
Romeo and Juliet, as well as a number of other favorite
passages he had. He held forth at lunch hours, and far from
discouraging him, the men would urge him on for more
and still more, listening appreciatively the while.

Mr. Worldly was the draftsman, dapper, pince-nezed,
and good-looking in a pale, thin-featured way. His name
was Harrison, and in the course of my father's attempts to
find some place where I'd fit in, I worked as his assistant
for a time—making blueprints for him (and, like as not,
overdeveloping them), transferring his drawings to tracing
paper (and occasionally ruining them, too)—and meantime listening, overawed, to the tales of his easy conquests.

I was at the prowling age, when I watched the girls
passing on the streets, speculating on their accessibility but
not daring to speak to them. Mr. Harrison had it easier than
that: it was the girls who spoke to him. And such girls! He
would hardly get downtown of a Saturday evening before
—"Well, there I was, at the corner of Clinton and Main,
just lighting a cigar, when she came up to me. Could I tell
her the way to the Seneca Theatre, she asked. I tipped my
hat, threw away my cigar, and said, certainly, certainly.
But since I was going that way myself . . ."

The girl usually turned out to be Marilyn Miller or Hazel

Dawn, or some other musical-comedy star of the day, on tour with her company, who had wandered afield and was now at her wit's end how to get back to the theater in time for the curtain. "Nowhere near as pretty as she looks on the stage. But then, who of them are?" he would add, out of his store of worldly wisdom, as I pictured him, gallantly cigarless, squiring the lady to her destination. The episode always ended with a supper at Odenbach's Rathskeller—*the* night spot of the period in Rochester—after the performance. What followed, he left to my imagination; it never occurred to me that a good part of the imaginings were his.

We had our Simple, a lathe hand, the cheerful butt of everyone, and our Goodman was the stockroom keeper, a tall, spare, white-haired man named MacLaren, who, in spite of the most outrageous provocation (people are always trying to play tricks on the stockroom keeper), had never been known to lose his temper in his life.

Our villain was a chunky, restless, black-haired, aggressive fellow called Bucky Connors, and I suppose I should be grateful to him, since it was directly because of him that my career as a mechanical engineer was canceled out for good. Or perhaps he was just my personal villain. At any rate, he just didn't like me, and there was something strangely disconcerting for a boy of my age then—or there was for me—to find himself confronted with active, unreasoned hostility. In a way, it was as if a bit of the ego, that round, protective, all-enveloping covering, had been lopped off, leaving an opening for all sorts of self-doubts and uncertainties to enter in. What had I done, what was wrong with me, to make him think so ill of me? And an enemy, an ill-wisher, can cause a lot of mischief in a small shop's close confines. There were the trippings, the bumpings off-balance as we passed in an aisle, the messings-up of jobs I was working on—and the inevitable half-mocking solicitude. "Oh, excuse me, kid! I didn't know you were there. You hurt?" Or, "Gee! I'm sorry. I thought you were through with that!"

I was a bit of a sissy in those days, I guess, at least as compared with a fellow of Bucky Connors's rough, tough background and pugnacious spirit. (He had a motorcycle, I remember, and aspired to be a boxer.) And his very contempt bred a kind of thwarted emulation in me; I used to daydream of drawing up alongside him on *my* motorcycle, both of us going about fifty—and then teasing him into a race: sixty, seventy, seventy-five, eighty, and then finally pushing her up to ninety as, baffled, he gave up and dropped back behind me. Or a feint with the left, then a right and another right . . . In or out of the shop, Bucky had me buffaloed.

Meantime, my progress as an embryonic mechanical engineer had been consistently downhill. As I've said, I didn't last long as Jess Griswold's helper; the truth was, he didn't have much need of me, or, I thought, much use for me, either. A toolmaker stands at the top of his craft because, as the name implies, he makes the tools, the templates, the molds, and other instruments that will later be used in actual manufacture; and in consequence his position is basic, since if he makes any mistakes, these will be repeated, and even magnified, all down the line.

He works alone, and mainly at the bench, since it's one of the paradoxes of the trade that the most delicate work is frequently done with the simplest of tools—a file, a handsaw, or even a piece of emery cloth being needed to reduce a shaft or a bearing to that final few thousandths of an inch of tolerance that assures a perfect fit. It was a job with a file that brought me to grief. As Mr. Griswold's helper, I'd spent most of my time doing odd jobs, the greater part of them unnecessary.

Like the surgeon's chief nurse at an operation, I would hand him a micrometer or a pair of calipers on demand, even if they were well within his reach if he'd wanted to reach for them, or I'd run to the stockroom for a bolt or a nut that he didn't have handy; I put away his tools in their proper places when he was done with them. The rest of the time I just stood around, or did what minor jobs he considered me capable of; and the filing job was one of these, for, as I still recall, all that I was asked to do was to smooth down the surface of a small cast-iron plate, preparing it for some other more delicate work to be done on it afterward.

In theory, I knew how to do the job, too, for Mr. Griswold, for all his crotchetiness, took his responsibilities as my instructor seriously, and he'd shown me many times the correct, indeed, the only way to use a file. "Flat to flat; that's the secret, boy," he'd say in his high, rather reedy, elderly voice. "And equal pressure throughout; otherwise, you'll round it or score it. You'll ruin it." And holding the file steadily at both ends in his hard-fleshed and deeply wrinkled but sensitive hands, he would stroke it delicately across the metal, to demonstrate. "There's one thing to remember, boy," he would usually add, for Mr. Griswold, though a taciturn man, was a mite sententious. "If a man can use a file, a breast drill, and a hack saw, he can make just about anything."

My father, I remember, used to say that it was a pleasure to watch an old-timer like Jess Griswold use a file; it was getting to be almost a lost art among the younger men. The trouble was that at that stage of my life I had no time for such esoterica. As I've said, my mind was on other things, and when Mr. Griswold gave me the filing job to do, I had hardly made more than a half-dozen swipes before I saw a telltale sliver of light across the face of the metal which showed that I'd scored it.

Mr. Griswold saw it, too. "No!" he cried, almost as if in pain, and he grabbed the file from my hands. "Look! Like this, boy!" He was just squaring away to give me one more lesson when he stopped and—I could see it coming up like a tide through his body to his face—a sense of the indignity he'd been about to submit himself to, wasting his time again after all the time he'd already wasted on me, rose up and flooded him. For a moment, his face seemed to swell and his body to tower, and I quaked, expecting a real outburst. Then he put the file down, very gently, on the bench. "You're just not interested, are you, boy?" he asked, and his tone was so quiet and reasonable that I had to answer him honestly.

"No," I said. "I guess I'm not, Mr. Griswold."

"Well, you can't teach a man things he don't want to learn," he said a bit heavily. "Guess we'll have to try to find out if there's anything you do want to know."

From then on—I suppose on the principle that it might help if I had a general grounding in machine work—I was shifted around a lot, winding up as a sort of part-time helper to everyone, with the emphasis, unfortunately, on the more tedious aspects of each operation. We were then, of course, far from automation as we know it now, but there were a good many things that could be done at least partly automatically. A job could be set up in a lathe or a shaper— turning down a shaft to a smaller dimension, let's say, or resurfacing a piece of metal—and an automatic feed engaged: my job then would be simply to watch, feeding oil occasionally to the moving parts, making sure that nothing loosened or went awry, till the cutting tool had reached the end of its travel, when my simple duty was to shut down the power, and then just stand around and wait until some more experienced hand either reset the tool for a deeper cut or set up another job for a similar operation.

It was easy work, certainly, and there were differences between the various machines that interested me vaguely: the high finicking whine of the drill press, for example, the dogged thrust and recoil of the shaper—really a sort of immensely powerful, mechanized plane, built for planing down metal instead of wood—the spit-and-polish gleam and glitter and somehow militant efficiency of a big lathe. They all have one common characteristic, however: monotony. I liked the lathe best of all, but, even there, there was something hypnotic in its spinning precision. It leads to daydreaming; it leads at times to a kind of euphoria, in which reason dissolves and one does the most foolish things without thinking of their danger. I was tending a lathe job one day, apparently in such a state, and what it led me to do was what seemed a harmless thing: I picked up a wrench and began trying it, idly, dreamily, on the bolt heads and nuts with which the frame of the lathe was studded.

I had tried all the bolts on the stationary parts of the lathe and I was still warming to my project. There remained a few more on the adjustment screws projecting from the head, or chuck; and this, of course, since it acts as a kind of rotating vise, holding the piece of metal to be turned, was in motion. It was turning, slowly to be sure, but it was turning, the tempting bolts revolving with it, and it should have been obvious to anyone in his right mind that if the wrench did fit on any of them it would be carried around inexorably to be jammed against the frame of the lathe beneath it. It was just at that moment that I heard the voice of the devil, Bucky Connors's voice behind me.

To be fair to him, I don't think he fully realized what he was getting me into, and, in any case, he was only echoing what was probably already in my bemused mind. Anyway, what he said was, "Whyn't you try it on the chuck?"

I did. I tried the wrench, and it fitted. It fitted all too well, and what happened after that was what was bound to happen. The wrench held, and on the instant—and with an abrupt, impersonal power that was terrifying—the lathe's motion was transferred to it, bringing it down and around, with my hand still clutching it, toward the heavy steel, motionless frame.

The rest, for a while, was pandemonium. I was still trying futilely to wrest the wrench free when I felt a blow on my wrist and a yank. I yanked, too, and my hand slipped free; simultaneously, it seemed, there was a grinding crash as the wrench handle hit the frame, cracked and bent; the lathe stopped, and there was a squeal of leather and a mighty flapping as the belt was thrown off the stalled pulley.

I turned, to find Mr. Griswold, still holding my arm, staring furiously at Bucky. "You did it, you damned little mischief maker!" Mr. Griswold was shouting. "You told him to do it! I heard you!"

"No, no, Mr. Griswold. You must have heard wrong," cried Bucky, and I had never seen him so discomfited. Faced with Mr. Griswold's anger, he was pale; he was practically stammering. "I never told him anything." Then, in desperation, he turned to me. "Did I, kid?" he asked, almost pleadingly.

And now both men were looking at me. My hand was intact, except for the forefinger. This was bleeding fairly copiously, but it hadn't begun hurting yet. It just felt numb, and I noticed that from all over the shop the other workmen were coming. I looked right back at Mr. Griswold and—I don't think it was noblesse oblige or any adolescent idea of that sort that moved me; I think, rather, it was an odd sort of feeling that I didn't want anyone to think that Bucky had been able to influence me in that fashion—I shook my head. "No, he didn't, Mr. Griswold," I said. "Or I didn't hear him. I just did it by myself."

Mr. Griswold glared at me, too, for a moment, then turned to Bucky. "If he'd lost his hand or his finger, young man, you'd have gone to jail for this. I'd have seen to it myself!" he said, then he turned to lead me to my father's little office. "Come on, boy. We've got to tend to this."

My father was away at the time on some business errand, but he came back a little later. Meantime, Bucky could hardly have been more solicitous. He followed us into the office, and it was he who ran to get the first-aid kit, he who heated some water for washing and stood by with bandages; it was he, finally, who ran out to the lathe and, backing the chuck off a little, released the wrench and discovered, caught between it and the frame, my fingernail, snatched off as I'd yanked my hand free.

It was a welcome discovery, for the forefinger had been mashed a little at the tip, and Mr. Griswold, afraid that the nail had been smashed along with it, had begun probing for it—I must say a bit painfully for me—and now he merely washed the wound, put on antiseptic, and bandaged it. In those easygoing, more or less infection-free days, it wasn't till evening—and then at my mother's insistence—that I was taken to see our family doctor.

The discovery of the fingernail served other purposes as well. At the shop, it was a visible evidence of how close the margin had been by which I escaped amputation, and I can still recall how the tiny, translucent hornlike fragment was passed from one hand to another, and pored over. At home, as I see it now, it turned out to be the margin, equally close, by which my father lost all chance for his "& Son," and I escaped forever from a career in mechanics.

When my father and I got home that night, we were a bit triumphant about my luck in avoiding disaster. My mother felt differently. "That boy is not going back in that shop again!" she said. "I'd be afraid every minute. It's too dangerous!" And—I don't know; my father was stubborn enough, but he was also extremely considerate where my mother was concerned; it may be, too, that Jess Griswold had had a word or two with him about my obvious lack of interest—anyway, he gave in, and when he did give in, he did it, as always, gracefully. I was never even asked to work in the shop again.

It must have puzzled him, however, for there were dozens of other families whose sons, the same age as I was, were growing up unquestioningly to go into the businesses —real estate, the law, optical equipment, dry-goods merchandising—that their fathers or even their grandfathers had established. And he must still have clung to some faint feeling of dynasty, for when he died, one of the things he left specifically to me was his tool chest, which he had preserved long after he'd had any practical use for it. It was a solid oaken chest, brass trimmed and dark with the dust and grease of many years' usage, with a hinged top opening on a recessed compartment and a series of shallow drawers beneath, lined with green baize, in which the tools were kept. And the majority of the tools were ones he had made himself as a youth, in the old-fashioned tradition, as a sign of his graduation from apprenticeship—scales, calipers, inside and out, and so on, right down to the micrometer, the last a precision instrument indeed, capable of measurements down to one-thousandth of an inch, or even smaller than the distance by which I didn't lose my finger.

I was married and living in the country by that time, and for a while I kept the tool chest on a workbench I had in the cellar. But I must have felt a little guilty about it even then, for it troubled me. It seemed wasted, just standing there, and I gave it finally to young Benjy French, the "& Son" of our local service station. It seemed to me that, in a way, he had more use for it, and more need, than I had.

 eleven

Essentially, they say, all wars are pretty much alike. They differ only in detail. But I confess that when I hear young men talk of flying nowadays, in terms of turbo-jet and jet, swept and delta wings, vertical take-off and so on, it is borne in on me that even the differences can be spectacular. I served my country for eight months or so, away back in 1918, as a Naval Aviation cadet (rank, Chief Quartermaster, Flight Status), and the fastest I ever flew in a plane with myself at the controls was one windy fall day at Bay Shore, Long Island, where we had our preliminary flight training.

The course we flew there was an elliptical one, covering Great South Bay from around Amityville to Patchogue, or some twenty miles on its longer axis, and the training planes we had were open-cockpit Curtiss biplanes, on single pontoons. They were powered by Hall-Scott engines, big, sturdy, four-cylinder affairs, heavy with cast iron and breathing out oil at every pore, and on the day I'm speaking of I made the run downwind in eleven minutes precisely, or at something just under one hundred and twenty miles an hour. The planes themselves had an air speed of only around eighty-five miles an hour, so the wind must have been blowing close to forty, and with my relatively small amount of experience I probably shouldn't have been up in such weather at all; I believe all flying was closed down for the day, shortly after. All I knew at the time was that I had the devil's own time coming back. I didn't care about that, though, for I had something to boast of for quite a while afterward. Close to two miles a minute! Boy!

That was fairly late in my career as an aviator, well after my first solo, and I'd had a few other exciting moments before that. First, of course, came Ground School, a dreary business, enlivened mainly by one incident which I still find memorable—this largely because it demonstrated to me for the first time, the old philosophical principle that a person is much more likely to be rewarded for acting badly, but interestingly, than for being uninteresting, but good.

We took our Ground School training at Cambridge, at the Massachusetts Institute of Technology, a number of whose buildings and the major part of whose campus had been taken over for the purpose, and it was the routine, mainly, that bored us. I suppose a good deal of all that has been changed by now and the training procedures, after both World War II and Korea, have been much more sensibly arranged. But, as I can realize now, at the time I'm speaking of the nation was engaged in what amounted to a pioneering enterprise. Not only were we involved in our first Great War; more than this, and scarcely more than five or six years earlier, flying itself had been a hit-or-miss, solitary adventure. You taught yourself, for the most part; indeed, a good many of the early flyers had built their own planes, or graduated from working as a mechanic on someone else's. And now, suddenly, the military and naval command had found itself faced with the necessity of training large masses of youngsters how to handle and fly and, if possible, understand an airplane—and in a hurry, too. I imagine the officers in charge of the program must have been almost as puzzled as anyone else about it. At any rate, they taught us some of the damnedest things.

A good deal of it, too, was surely influenced by that ancient military maxim: Keep them busy. What we got, anyway, in addition to a certain amount of preflight instruction, was a mishmash compounded, I'd guess, of curriculum at Annapolis and the training given to the ordinary seaman. The preflight instruction itself, it still seems to me, was sound enough, though even here there were a few frills around the edges. We took engines apart and put them together again. We disassembled and reassembled machine guns, learning the nomenclature in the process; we had lectures on aerodynamics and learned the principles of navigation. On the lunatic side, we had sessions in a big, high-ceilinged hall, with an enormous map of the English Channel covering the entire floor and little simulated cockpits spaced along a balcony above, where we could practice wireless telegraphy and drop imaginary bombs. It was designed, I suppose, to get us used to "action in the air." Link trainers, I understand, do the whole thing much better now.

For the naval part of it, we learned the flag signal code and had lectures on seamanship. We had target practice and small-arms drill; we had foot drill, marching to the slow Navy cadence, and once, just so we would know the facts of life, we were taken en masse to Boston Navy Yard and given a tour of a battleship. Most improbable of all, to my mind at least, we even had small-boat drill on the Charles, rowing up and rowing down, shipping oars and so on, while a boatswain's mate shouted orders. ("Damn it all, they *are* in the Navy, aren't they?" I can imagine some Washington admiral bellowing, if anyone had the temerity to ask how learning to ship our oars in unison was going to affect our proficiency as flyers.)

We had eight weeks of this, in all, and it was toward the end of that time that the incident I spoke of earlier occurred. Classes graduated from Ground School every two weeks, and in our last two weeks we, like all those in the classes preceding us, were quartered in a separate building, for a bit more intensive training. There we were commanded—perhaps "brooded over" is a better term—by an officer who in his own way seemed to us somewhat special, too.

For one thing, he was a full lieutenant, whereas most of the other officers we had had to do with had been J.G.'s or even ensigns. He had his wings, too, which gave him glamour, since we longed for them so much ourselves. Otherwise, he was short, but solidly built (rather like a quarterback, which, I believe, he had been, before leaving college), and cocky, with a rather handsome but sullen face. I guess he hated to be there, grounded as he was like any Kiwi (our slang for a nonflying officer), for he paid as little attention as possible to the whole damn business of running the station.

Until, that is, one day when at the usual parade of the colors at sundown, he appeared, to review and then dismiss us, with none other than Frances White as his guest for the occasion. I imagine a bit of back-dating is needed at this moment. Miss White was a small, bouncy, pert, pretty girl who had made a name for herself in musical comedy for her "little girl" roles. She always dressed like a twelve-year-old, in pigtails, big ribbon bows, and the briefest possible pinafores—a costume, or role, that somehow seemed more enticing to the elders in the audience then than it might be now—and she was especially famous for her "Mississippi" song ("M-I-S-S-I-S-S-I-P-P-I"). Though we knew she was playing in Boston in some show or other at the time, we had never connected her with our little lieutenant. There she was, though, standing smiling beside him, to review us, and with our newly developed *esprit de corps* I believe we all felt that his triumph was ours as well: the march past we gave her at the end was the snappiest in all our brief history.

So we thought, anyway. But our commandant, the lieutenant, thought differently, or he came to some such conclusion as the rest of the evening wore on. Lights-out for us was at nine, but that did not apply to him, apparently, as we learned when around one o'clock, or even later (we were all too sleepy and confused to notice the time), we were aroused by a bugle blast and a sudden turning on of all the lights, and we turned over blinking in our bunks to see the lieutenant standing, it may be a little unsteadily, on a desk near the dormitory doorway, staring angrily down at us.

"Attent-*shun!*" he called, and we all scrambled down from our bunks. Since he gave us no "at ease" afterward, we stood there, stiffly, while for a quarter of an hour or so he told us, in scathing detail, how inept we had been, and still were, how slew-footed and dull-witted; what a disgrace we had been—not only to him and the station, but to Miss White and American womanhood as well—in the review; and how hopeless we were as real officer material generally.

There was muttering about it afterward. Naval aviation was in those days a kind of club. I have no figures, but I don't believe the total personnel could have numbered more than ten thousand men, with perhaps a couple of thousand of them officers, and the whole service branch had not been in operation more than a few years at the time I got into it. The result was that everyone, officers and cadets alike, was pretty much of an age—the ensigns, for instance, being simply fellows who had left college to enter the service six months or so before we had (a college background, as I remember, was one of the conditions for entrance), while the higher-ranking men, in most instances, were only slightly older.

This was the case, too, with our commandant, and our principal mutterings centered on a feeling that he had been "showing off"; like an upperclassman riding a bunch of freshmen too hard, he'd been getting beyond his age. But he was an officer still, and hence endowed—or so in our fevered minds we imagined him to be—with practically the power of life and death over us. Though we felt he had been unjust to us, we awaited further developments fearfully. When, a few days later, an orderly told us the commandant wanted to see me, I approached the door of his office fairly apprehensively.

He was seated at his desk when I entered, and he did not look up when I saluted, announced my name, and stood at attention. "At ease," he said almost absently, but he still stared down at his desk for a moment or two. When he raised his head, I was surprised at the look on his face. It was a mixture of sullenness, exasperation, and sheer woefulness, and I was still more surprised when he came out with a full apology.

I can't recall now all he said, but I do remember it came out haltingly and, as it were, ungraciously—but all this, clearly, was because he hated doing it at all. "I just wanted to say it was a damn-fool thing I did the other night," he said, or something like that, in the bitten-off, rasping voice he had. "It wasn't you fellows' fault; it was mine. I was tight, God damn it, and I shouldn't have been. Or if I was, I shouldn't have shown it."

Then he stopped and looked me over, almost balefully. As I see it now, he was trying to reconcile his status as an officer, and hence as a personage automatically above reproach, with his obligations as a decent human being, and being fairly new to the problem, too, he still wasn't able to manage it gracefully. "I'm doing this to every damn man on the station. Dismissed!" he snarled, and looked down at his desk again. As I went out, I heard the orderly calling another name.

In all fairness, I suppose that should have been the end of the matter. He had wronged us, and he had made amends; things were even on both sides. The outcome, however, was different. As I've said, all this happened toward the end of Ground School, and—I suppose as a symbol of our growing up, into not only adult but naval life—it was the custom for each graduating class to celebrate with a big dinner, off station, and very manlike and roisterous, on the night before leaving for flight training. The commandant attended ours; I imagine it was almost a part of his duties. And—I don't know; he'd been gruff, he'd been grouchy, he'd been ungracious. He had robbed us of pretty much a whole night's sleep—a precious thing indeed, in view of the daily schedule we had—and even in apologizing he had managed to make us feel that, damn it, it was partly our fault.

And yet the fact was, he *had* apologized, and that, somehow, humanized him; more than that, it showed that he'd had us on his conscience, he really cared. Anyway, what we did—and to his surprise: indeed, I don't think I've ever seen a more surprised man in my life—was to present him with a wrist watch, a darned good one, too, suitably engraved, and tendered as a token of our esteem and regard, and so on. For a while, he just stared at it.

"What the hell is this for?" he demanded, and then—and this showed he appreciated the paradox involved, for we would surely never have thought of the gesture if it hadn't been for our little nocturnal encounter—he added, still wonderingly, "You guys must be nuts!"

But he rose to the occasion, rose literally, too, for he got up, strapping on the wrist watch as he did so, and made a brief oration. "But I'll wear it, damn it. I'll wear it, and be proud of it, too. You were a pretty good bunch, and I'm proud of you, too." Then he reached for his glass. "Here's to you! Let's hope you don't wind up back in this hellhole, like me!"

That was Ground School. Flight training was different. Our whole class couldn't have numbered more than fifty cadets, in those small-scale days, and about a third of these had opted for lighter-than-air, or for training in blimps, dirigibles, and balloons. So I suppose there were only about thirty of us who went from Boston to New York and then to the flight station at Bay Shore—shepherded, incidentally, by a real Navy petty officer, a bosun's mate, whom we all outranked but who still, apparently, was considered better able than any of us to supervise the journey. We arrived fairly late in the day, and my first sight of the station, and the planes in the sky, is something I'm sure I shall never, really, forget.

It was hastily built, as most wartime installations are, an unprepossessing jumble of hangars, workshops, barracks, and other buildings set down in the sand dunes along the shore, and we were lined up in front of the administration building (actually a converted summer cottage) waiting to be checked in when a formation of three planes came by. I saw them only briefly, as they passed on the other side of the hangars, but just then the leader dove and then zoomed a little. He did it three or four times, followed by the others, and I learned later on that it was merely the signal to break formation. But at the moment, I thought that the sight of those three planes, swooping in unison like swallows, was one of the loveliest things I'd ever seen in my life. As a matter of fact, I still do.

My first flight, though, was almost a catastrophe. On signing into the station, we were assigned, more or less by rote, to one or another of the instructors on duty there, and I drew one named Ensign Scott, or perhaps, rather, he drew me. He was a tall, lean, lantern-jawed fellow, dark-haired and dark-eyed, and, like so many of the other officers I ran into, obviously bored with it all and aching to get overseas; and my induction, up to a point at least, followed what I'm sure was to him the usual pattern, though for me it was an exciting one.

Between flights (between? At this stage I hadn't even had *one* yet!), we were quartered, in groups of a half-dozen or so, with our joint instructor, in little open-faced sheds spaced out along the beach at either side of the hangars. A plane would land and come taxiing in, to ground its pontoon gently, like a boat, in the sand before us. A student would climb out of the rear cockpit (the instructor always rode in the front one) and a couple of mechanics would check the plane over quickly; the instructor—in my case, of course, Ensign Scott—would call out the name of the student next in order. I imagine this phase of flight training must have been considerably speeded up, too, in these tenser times. I hope so, for the flying-by-turns method practiced then, when one was still under instruction and had not soloed, was obviously a time-consuming procedure. The greater part of the time, we were like substitute ball-players, sitting in the dugout and watching the progress of a game in which we had no part; and by the time my turn came, that first day on the beach, I was already long gone in a state, not of fear—for I somehow assumed, from the start, that I'd surely be able to fly—but of mingled anxiety, anticipation, and frustration.

I climbed into the cockpit, or was boosted, and in a daze went through a brisk, preliminary indoctrination. The throttle here, at the right; turn and bank indicator in the dash before you, as well as altimeter, air-speed indicator, and oil gauge; that was about the sum of our instruments in those days. Army training planes, then as now, had a movable post called the "joy stick," working on a swivel, to operate all the flight controls. The Navy, naturally, was different. *We* had a wheel control, called the Deperdussin, and very like the ones in use on airliners today; it was mounted on a movable post, too, but the post moved only forward and back, to lower or raise the tail fins and so lose or gain altitude, while in a turn you used the wheel like any steering wheel, to operate the ailerons and so dip the wings in one direction or another. The rudder in the tail assembly, which initiated the turn, was operated by a rudder bar, on the floor at your feet.

I'm not sure if my description is clear; certainly, at that first try, it was only partly so to me, and I go into it at such length here only because of the part it played in later developments. But by now the mechanics had shoved us off the beach and turned us tail to the shore; Ensign Scott taxied out into the bay and then idled the engine a few moments, while the plane turned head into the wind. And it was a bright, brisk, beautiful day, blue-skied and just breezy enough to set the ripples slapping against the pontoon and give the air a touch of salt from the spray. The planes then, too—wooden-strutted and canvas-covered, wire-stayed and open-cockpitted—had, for all their awkwardness, a kind of immediacy of contact about them. They weren't insulated, they weren't pressurized; once you were in the air, you damned well knew you were flying.

As I say, Ensign Scott idled there for a moment. Then, suddenly, he hit the throttle, and I had for the first time a practical demonstration of the wonders of aerodynamics. Fundamentally, and for all the classroom work I'd had on the subject, I still couldn't quite believe—in a sense, I still can't believe—that a simple stick of wood or metal, beating against the empty air, can haul a huge contraption like an airplane up into the skies and around in them. Yet, here before my eyes, it was doing it, the plane sloshing heavily along at first, its pontoon deep in the water; then up on the step and scooting; and then, abruptly—as invariably happens, we were a couple of hundred feet up before I realized what had happened—airborne at last, the wires humming companionably, the wings taut, and a general feeling of everything right and in its proper element at last.

Ensign Scott took me up to around five thousand feet (at which point, I remember, the whole station looked so small that I wondered how we'd ever be able to get down to it again), put me through some acrobatics, just to let me know what it was all about, and then waggled the stick a couple of times—as he'd already told me, the sign that I was to take over.

And so there I was, away up in the sky, in charge of things; I must admit it was a little disconcerting. I hadn't realized, I guess, that, as with a car, the only way to learn to fly a plane is to fly one, and the easy confidence I'd felt on the beach began disintegrating. Scott, though, seemed to have no such qualms about the matter. Having given up the controls, he had apparently given up all concern about everything. He had even slumped down in his seat a little; from where I sat, he looked precisely like a man settling down for a quiet nap.

He had clearly left things up to me; rather gingerly, I grabbed the wheel and for a time, surprisingly, had no trouble. The thing flew. All I had to do was to sit still, and it flew! It wasn't till we got down around Babylon, near the end of our course, that I got into trouble. We had to turn there to follow our prescribed elliptical course, and, sure enough, Scott's hand rose lazily out of the cockpit ahead of me, as had been arranged, to signal the turn.

The only difficulty was that by now I'd got bemused by the ease of it all. I'd driven cars, of course, and now with the familiar feel of the wheel in my hands I turned as one would a car, completely forgetting the rudder. I won't try to describe the aerodynamics of the situation, and certainly I didn't understand them then. All I knew was that in seconds the wind was slapping my face in gusts, the nose of the plane was pointed down, and the tail was whipping around and around erratically; as I learned later, we were in a spin, and an instant later Scott took over.

I might add, too, as a further instance of the pioneering character of the period, that if this had happened only a few years earlier, it would almost certainly have meant the end for both Ensign Scott and me. A tail spin is a curious maneuver. Though the nose is pointed down and the plane is falling, it is actually in a stall; and although the instinctive tendency is to pull back on the controls, in an effort to level off, the only way to get out of the predicament is to push forward, accentuating the dive, before doing anything else to get out of it.

Until someone, probably by accident, discovered this paradoxical state of affairs, planes, once in a spin, had just kept on spinning, their pilots fighting the controls until they crashed. As it was, though, we had altitude, which is another necessary ingredient. And I suppose I was maybe Scott's fiftieth, even his hundredth flyer, and he'd already found himself in this very same spot, perhaps a dozen times along the line. He put the nose down, straightened out the controls, and, well short of disaster, leveled us off again.

"What the hell'd you think you were driving, a Hupmobile?" he demanded, when we'd taxied in to the beach at the end.

So, eventually, we fitted into the new routine. There was an early-morning flight—before breakfast, even—which most of us detested, for by now it was mid-autumn, and at that time of day it was cold. Then there was a morning session of classes, in which we disassembled and reassembled engines, machine guns, and so on all over again, and delved further, and with more understanding now, into the mysteries of flight theory, astronomy, and elementary navigation. Afternoons, we flew again, and that was the best of the lot.

As I look back on it now, we had a dedicated, one might say even a martyr's feeling about our new vocation. The war—the real, fighting war; the war of mud and trenches, shells and gas and rifle fire—was at least three thousand miles away from us; and our nearest approach to it, even with luck, would be a job patroling the English Channel, which was what our branch, being of the Navy, was principally assigned to do.

Yet for all that, we managed to get pretty darned ro-

mantic about the perils that confronted us. Someone, I remember, had come upon a not too optimistic estimate of the
chances of survival the members of each branch could expect. Unless I'm wrong, and at this late date I may well be,
machine gunners, since they were supposed to cover any
retreat, were the worst off; they had an average of about
thirty days of battle apiece to look forward to. (I might
add, without levity, that a classmate of mine died, as a
machine gunner, well within that estimate.) Infantrymen
had something like ninety days' chance of survival, and
artillerymen still more. A flyer had about fifty—or so our
anonymous authority had said—and this possibly question-
able statistic filled us with a mixture of gloom and fascination. We felt doomed, as well as dedicated, and it helped
a lot with the girls we met at parties on weekend liberty
in New York.

Mostly, though, the mood was hopeful. We were too
young to feel that we *could* die, really, and I know that my
own brushes with danger, or even the sight of it, were few.
Now and then, sitting on the beach between flights, we
would see a plane come diving or spinning down—down,
down, and down, while we all held our breaths, till it
passed that invisible horizon line in the sky, about a thousand feet above the real one, which meant that it was no
longer possible for the pilot to pull out in time to avoid
a crash.

This happened perhaps a half-dozen times in the course
of my stay at the station, and each time, while we waited
and watched till the plane went in, and then waited again
while the crash boat raced out to pick up the pieces, each
time, one was likely to have a few quick moments when the
feeling of death, still and chill and somber, would intervene
before the bright sun and sea and sky. But the old planes,

for all their cloth and baling-wire construction, were surprisingly resilient. We had only one funeral in all the five or six weeks I was at Bay Shore.

I had a few bad moments myself. Great South Bay, our field of operations, was a long-established haunt of duck hunters, and, war or no war, they were not of a mind to give up their prerogatives lightly. When the duck season opened, they swarmed out there, regardless of the fact that the area was officially a naval reservation (I don't think the Navy, or the military in general, had so much *authority* then as now); and, in consequence, as I was taking off one misty morning, after a practice landing, I was barely airborne when I looked down from the cockpit and saw a party of hunters, crouched in almost Grecian attitudes of terror, in a rowboat not more than thirty feet below me.

In the planes of those days, with the engine mounted before you, high in the nose, you didn't have much forward visibility, particularly at take-off, and since they'd been directly in front of me, I just hadn't seen them before; furthermore, they had no business being there, anyway. I could understand how they must have felt, though, sitting helplessly in the path of an oncoming plane, rushing at them out of the mist. They were scared and, to be honest about it, so was I, at the thought of what havoc there might have been if the old Hall-Scott hadn't lifted me just in time.

Once, too, I had a brush with another plane, which for some reason was flying in the direction opposite to mine. That was odd, all round, for our rules about flying practice were precise. As I've already said, we flew counterclockwise, around the rim of the bay. En route, we were supposed to practice landings and take-offs; when we'd mastered them, we went on to spirals and fixed landings (which

meant landings near a given target), and then, finally, formation flying and aerobatics. The other pilot, maybe, had
gotten confused in a spiral. Anyway, there I was, sailing
along in that wonderfully euphoric mood that flying can
bring about in one—dreaming, possibly of Fonck or Guy-
nemer or of Lufberry, and wondering if the name of Coates
would ever be added to that list—when, before I knew it,
here was another plane, like a phantom emanation from the
skies over the Ardennes, like Von Richtofen himself,
coming straight at me!

I luffed, or whatever you'd call it, to the right, and the
other fellow, fortunately, to the left. But we passed so
close that it made my head swim, and I sat down immediately for a landing, to think things over. I had often
wondered what it felt like to aim your plane straight at
another and hold it there into close-firing range, as the
real fighting pilots had to do all the time. Now I knew,
and it didn't make me feel any happier.

The whole thing ended, more or less, with the Armistice, and I feel sorry for anyone too young to have experienced the first one. On the last one, V-J Day, my wife
and I were walking down West Eleventh Street, in New
York, when we heard the deep, distant, but steadily rising
roar—first of boat whistles in the harbor and then of sirens
and horns everywhere—that signaled the news. Later, we
spent the evening wandering in Chinatown and Little Italy,
and Lord knows it was gay enough; there was dancing in
the street all up and down Mulberry Street.

But it still couldn't compare with the first one, which, incidentally, was the "false" one. It was about noon, as I
recall, that the news came into the station, and our commandant gave us liberty for the day almost immediately.
(Since he never woke us up for any midnight lectures, I

can't even recall what he looked like now, or anything else about him.)

We all took the first train we could get to New York, but it was evening by the time we got there. We ran into what amounted to city-wide pandemonium, with ourselves —with, that is, anyone and everyone in uniform—as its roving centers. It was startling at first. We'd come in from the disciplined orderliness of a Naval installation. We hadn't known what to expect; and I think no one in the city, either, individually, had anticipated what the sudden snapping of the massed tensions and anxieties of the war would result in, in the way of collective expression. What I remember, mostly, is a sea of shouting faces, wave on wave and street on street of them, laughing, cheering, singing—with, here and there, scattered episodes standing out.

I had teamed up with a fellow cadet named Charlie Hohner—no great friend, particularly; we'd just found ourselves together in the hurly-burly that greeted us even in Long Island Station—and at my suggestion we soon headed for Greenwich Village. This was because I had already discovered that it was an art center, and on previous visits to the city I'd prowled about there hopefully, looking for artists, bohemianism, and, possibly, wickedness, and, though I'd found no wickedness to speak of, it had become pleasantly familiar territory. Now, however, its easy, bohemian quality had vanished, swallowed up in the celebrative mood, or, to put it another way, a great wave of pagan merriment had spread over the entire city, engulfing the Village along with it. We were hailed, we were seized, we were kissed in the Village, but we were also seized and kissed everywhere else, and swept into dancing circles, and toasted.

I can see now that we were only symbols, and the mood,

for all its wantonness, was primarily beatific. We were not real heroes, we were only putative ones, but we were there to be fondled and grabbed at; we would do till the real ones, maybe even the grabbers' sons, came back. And, meantime, this was not simply the end of *a* war, it was the end of a war to *end* wars—hadn't President Wilson said so himself?—and the feeling everywhere was that a true Golden Age was at last at hand.

At the moment, though, I felt embarrassed and guilty. In the first place, I had, but this time on a massive scale, that disconcerted sensation a youngster always has when he's among a group of older people who have simply gone out of control. In addition, our responsibility to the uniform, as soon-to-be officers and gentlemen, had been drilled into us so thoroughly that I'm afraid I had a certain compunction about that: all this pulling about and hail-fellowing seemed somehow degrading, most particularly when I thought how little I'd done in the war as compared with the men who were still in combat, or had died in it, overseas.

I think in general we uniformed noncombatants were solemner, that Armistice night, than the civilians were; we weren't heroes, but we'd hoped to be heroes some day (if possible, of course, painlessly), and this certainly meant the end of that. I remember pulling away, I guess a little testily, from a man who'd accosted me in a Village restaurant, and pointing out to him that I hadn't really shot down any enemy planes yet, I hadn't even done any fighting; I was still just a student pilot, and now that was probably all I'd ever be.

It didn't matter a bit to him. " 'S Okay. You would, boy, when the time came. You'd do all right," he told me, and his wife, in a transport, rushed over and kissed me.

All this almost austerely disapproving attitude on my

part, I must admit, was confined to the earlier part of the evening, for it was in that same restaurant that Hohner and I met the Army pilot. As a consequence, the first Armistice night is memorable to me for still another reason. It was the night when I first got drunk.

The Army pilot was a tall, lanky fellow, quite tight, and Hohner and I met him in a corridor of the restaurant, coming back from the men's room. And I guess the carnival spirit was by that time beginning to take hold of us, too, for as we passed him I heard myself saying, on impulse, "I wish we were feeling the same way you do."

Nothing simpler, he told us at once. "Just go down to the corner below the restaurant, and you'll find a bunch of kids there. Give them a few bucks and they'll get you a bottle. Enjoy yourselves!" And he gave us a wave of the hand and went weaving on into one of the dining rooms.

So, we did. We went down to the corner, and, sure enough, there were three or four tough-looking kids clustered under the arc light. Sure enough, they said that if we gave them the money they would get us a bottle. We got up three dollars between us, which was about all we could afford, and they darted off instantly, still in a group, down the side street.

Charlie Hohner and I watched them go and then glanced at each other: there, we thought, went our three dollars. As it turned out, though, we were mistaken. This was Armistice night, a time when amity prevailed, and as proof of it I can record the fact that within minutes the kids were back not only with a pint of whisky, but with change. We thanked them, and went across the street and down it a little way to a sort of service passage, between buildings, to consider the matter, and the bottle.

At this point, a few difficulties arose. In my own case,

both my parents were nondrinkers. There had never been any liquor in the house while I was with the family, and since leaving it, I had been most of the time in uniform, and so under the rulings of the War-Time Prohibition Act, that strange regulation which decreed that, though civilians could drink all they wanted to, servicemen—for purity, supposedly—couldn't. More than that, it had somehow just never occurred to me to drink, and now it turned out that Hohner, a big, blond, gentle fellow from Kansas, was in the same innocent category.

Here we were, though, with a bottle of whisky and both of us committed to carnival. I forget which one of us unstoppered the bottle, but whichever it was, he took a gulp, swallowed down a cough, and passed it to the other, who gulped in turn and passed it back again. We repeated the process once more and then glanced at each other questioningly.

"Do you feel anything?" Hohner asked, and I shook my head; I must admit that, again unfairly, doubts about the probity of our young bootleggers passed through my mind. The stuff tasted awful enough to be whisky, certainly, but *was* it whisky? Or was it some cheap, harmless substitute? We'd both had the idea that whisky took effect immediately, and here—and even after a couple more gulps apiece —it wasn't. It just wasn't doing *anything* to us, and it wasn't until we had finished the pint between us that the first sensations of dreamy, drunken unsteadiness began to come over us.

After that, everything got progressively fuzzier. I do recall that, a half hour or so later, the two of us were leading a kind of snake-dance parade to a night club of the era called "The Black Cat," though how the parade got started or what happened afterward—even, if we got into "The

Black Cat" at all—is now lost to me forever. In the same random way, I have no recollection of how Hohner and I got back to the station at all.

In a sense, it hardly mattered. For soon after that—very soon, in our case, for, as I've said, Naval Aviation was then a very small branch of the service, and easily manipulated— we were all being processed for retirement to the reserve and demobilization. I was back at college well before the Christmas holidays.

I could have stayed in, of course, as a few did. But I didn't, and in consequence I've always had a sort of truncated feeling about that phase of my life, a feeling of unfulfillment. I'd been aiming for my wings, and I never got them; I'd have had to do some training in the big, lumbering old flying boats, called H-Boats, beforehand, and at the time it seemed ridiculous. And there was, underneath it all, a feeling of pointlessness about everything: the war we'd all joined up for was over, and from now on anything we did would be done to a different purpose from the one we'd started out with—for that matter, to no purpose at all, but in a kind of spiritual vacuum.

In the end, my career as an aviator began to take on an aspect almost of the illusory. I never saw our Boston commandant again, but I hope he still has his watch tucked away somewhere; in fact, we dispersed so far and so fast that I've seen very few of my old comrades in arms since then. I did see Ensign Scott, my old instructor, though, and not long after our demobilization. I ran into him on Church Street, in New Haven; he was in civilian clothes, and at first I didn't recognize him. But it turned out that he was at Yale, too, over in the Scientific School. In fact, he was only a couple of years ahead of me, and though this reduced him a little in my estimation (I had thought that he, at *least*, was older), I was still deferential. He, for once, was complimentary.

"You should have stayed in," he said, and it's one of the remarks I treasure. "You might have made a pretty good flyer."

But then, I might have asked, why hadn't he stayed in himself? I didn't, though. For one thing, I wanted to get away before he said something that might "take back" that last remark of his. From the saturnine Scott, it had been practically an accolade.

 twelve

Monte Rosa is not the highest peak in the Alps, nor is it the most difficult. Mont Blanc tops it by more than five hundred feet (15,781 as against 15,217, though how they get their measurements so exact at such lofty altitudes has always been beyond me), while most mountaineers, I believe, regard the Dent Blanche and the Matterhorn, among others, as harder to climb. Still, Monte Rosa is a fairly rugged mountain. Edward Whymper, the man who first conquered the Matterhorn, speaks of it with respect; and even William Conway, a man so indefatigable that he once made a kind of marathon tour of the Alps, starting in the south at the Italian border and climbing each peak that confronted him till he reached the Tyrol, or some twenty mountains in all—even Conway has a careful word to say about the great fields of glaciers, crevasse-riddled, that guard Monte Rosa's summit.

That Monte Rosa, however, the Alpine one, is not the Monte Rosa I had to do with. The one I climbed, or almost climbed, is a small peak of only some eight thousand feet in the center of the island of Corsica; and I learned to my surprise, in the course of some brief checking-up I did in preparation for this account, that it isn't even called Monte Rosa, though because of some mental mix-up, I'd been for years under the impression that it was!

Mine, I've discovered, is the Monte Rotondo. But by whatever name one calls it, it is still a mountain, equipped with such Alpine features as considerable areas of steep rocky slopes and clifflike escarpments, a series of sharp arêtes leading up to the summit and—for all its position in mid-Mediterranean—a sizable cap of permanent snow and ice at the top. My attempt on it was undertaken away back in the middle nineteen-twenties, and I'm sure would have been completely successful if my companion on the trip, an artist friend of mine named Wynn Holcomb, hadn't lost his walking stick when we were only a few hundred yards from the summit.

On the other hand, if Wynn *hadn't* lost his walking stick in the way he did, we might easily have met with real disaster. But perhaps by now a little backtracking is in order—some of which, for people who didn't grow up in the period I'm speaking of, may be a bit difficult to assimilate.

Let no one be surprised, for instance, that Wynn carried a walking stick—instead of, let's say, an alpenstock—on our expedition. I hope I won't stretch credulity beyond the limit if I add that he also wore patent-leather dress oxfords, a double-breasted black suit with a voluminous jacket, and a wide-brimmed black velours hat as well—and had worn them all through a three- or four-day walking trip we'd made on the island, before our essay into mountain climbing. In them, he looked like someone who had strayed from *La Vie de Boheme* by way of Broadway. But it was the way he dressed on the Boulevard Montparnasse, and he saw no reason to change it for the Corsicans.

Wynn was one of the true eccentrics, in a period when

they abounded; he was picturesque even in Paris. But, for all his garb, we were in Corsica, at least partly, for the laudable purpose of making some money. Short, brisk, wiry, impish, and volatile, extravagant in his gestures as in his imagination, and for all his prankishness an infinitely beguiling companion, Wynn had come over to Paris a year or so earlier with the idea of having what turned out to be a rather desultory try at oil painting. But he was also an accomplished illustrator, and in that capacity he and I (as the writing member of the team) had already eked out our separate income by collaborating on a number of Sunday-magazine pieces for the newspapers back home—most of them about Paris and its environs, with a few excursions elsewhere.

And Corsica was in the news at the moment, because of the activities of a romantic young bandit whose name I can no longer recall, but whose photograph—curly-haired, grinning, and loaded with weapons and bandoleers—still remains in my mind as it appeared in the Paris dailies. He had killed a policeman, or committed some other unpardonable crime, and all France was following his pursuit, as the *gendarmerie* tried to track him down in the maqui. Now a hopeful editor had decided that New York might be interested, too, and commissioned a couple of stories on the place.

Though we'd seen no bandits as yet, and indeed had only a minimal desire to, it had turned out to be an extremely interesting excursion. Corsica, I learn from an ancient Baedeker I've just dug up, is only about a hundred miles long by some fifty at its widest part. But for all its relatively small size, it is almost incredibly varied, both in scenery and in general atmosphere. This derives in large part, I think, from its topography, which is very rugged, with the few fertile areas separated one from another by steep spines and rocky ridges, running up to the three or four central peaks. Communications are primitive, too, or they were when I was there, and the result is a kind of segmented life, with little or no contact even between one valley and the next.

You got some really startling contrasts. Ile Rousse, the town where Wynn and I had landed from Marseille, had not only the look but the very atmosphere of a typical Provençal village—a wide, sheltered bay, with the blue-green waters of the Mediterranean lap-lapping lazily against a long stone *quai*, and the town built around a big, shady central *place*, itself surrounded by awninged cafés. We'd gone next to Bastia, at the northern tip of the island, and here the aspect of things was as sternly narrow-streeted, stone-fronted, and grim as that of Genoa, just across from it, on the mainland; while Ajaccio, farther south, where we went from Bastia, was by contrast almost tropical. Here huge eucalyptus trees lined the streets and their fragrance filled the air; many of the houses had vine-covered wrought-iron porches, and the town was somno-lent by day while at night the deserted streets and cafés filled suddenly, little string orchestras started playing everywhere, and there was even a formal promenade along the sidewalks enclosing the main plaza—the women, often with flowers stuck in their hair in the traditional fashion, walking one way and the men the other. Porto, a town hardly more than thirty miles down the coast from Ile Rousse but separated from it by a series of rocky ridges and gorges, was curiously Greek in character, with squat stone-and-stucco houses, tile-roofed, and narrow, cobble-stoned streets along which goatherds were constantly marshaling their flocks out to the fields and back again. It was supposed to have been settled by a colony of Greek adventurers, away back in the Middle Ages, and because of its relative isolation had remained more or less as they had made it.

At this distance in time, I can't recall precisely why we decided to try to climb Monte Rotondo. It was there, of course, and so were we at the moment. I had always had a secret desire to do some real mountaineering, preferably in the Alps (which, I suppose, psychologically, may well be the reason why our little Corsican peak got so thoroughly confused with the great Monte Rosa in my mind), and here at least was a chance at a minor essay. Mostly, though, I think it was because the innkeeper expected us to. The inn was outside the town of Vizzavona, at the edge of a pine wood, I remember, and we had stopped there for the night in the course of a little walking trip we were making from Ajaccio up into the interior.

I won't go into too much detail about the walking trip. It was fun, as any such excursion is if you are young and have the leisure for it, and the weather is good and the country attractive, as Corsica undeniably is. The whole island, it seems, geologically, is actually a continuation of the great Alpine chain. It's the tip of a huge peak, or a group of them, submerged, which accounts for its ruggedness, and it rises steadily from the coast to the really mountainous region at the center, the roads winding and zigzagging, usually with a fast-running little stream alongside, up the valleys or around the ridges between.

The country was very much wilder than in France—to the point that at times, traversing some especially desolate region, we would more than half expect to see some bandit staring down at us over his rifle sights from his lookout among the rocks above—and the towns were a little farther apart. But they were close enough so that we were never at a loss for a meal, or a drink (the wine bottle filled straight from the tun, in the cool, dim wine cellar) or a night's lodging; and the people, though a little gruff at first meeting, were surprisingly cordial.

More than that, and unlike the French—at that time, at any rate—they seemed perfectly able to understand that a man might go on a walking trip just for the fun of it. By the French, it was taken for granted that the only reason anyone would travel afoot was that he couldn't afford any more comfortable means of transportation; and by all but the members of the younger generation of *les sportifs*, then just arising, the traveler afoot was regarded with suspicion in consequence. To be sure, the Corsicans themselves didn't walk much, if they could help it. Mostly, they went mule- or donkey-back, which, though equally slow, at least kept your feet off the ground.

But they had no objection to other people's walking, and in a roundabout way I think the fact that Corsica, and particularly Ajaccio, was a favorite winter resort for the British was responsible. For the British *do* like walking, and they've also always been known for their bland, invincible way of imposing their own customs on whatever other country they happen to be in. So in Corsica, as I imagine it, they *walked*, as they'd have walked in Dorset or Sussex, and the natives could damn well get used to it—as certainly, in our case, they were, for we were treated with respect, and even with deference, everywhere along the way.

Or Wynn was, at any rate, for it occurs to me now, too, that Wynn's cane and his elaborate attire may have had a share in the outcome, though it operated a little to my disadvantage. For if Wynn's tastes ran to the dandiacal, mine were the opposite. I went in then for rough clothes, flannel shirts and workingmen's boots; I also carried the rucksack,

and it must have seemed obvious to the villagers we encountered that here they were confronted not only with
an Englishman indulging his strange passion for slogging
afoot cross-country but by one who did it in the grand
manner, dressed for Bond Street and with his personal
servant to carry his marching equipment. There were times,
at any rate, when I thought I detected a look of surprise
on an innkeeper's face, when he saw that Wynn permitted
me to sit down at the table with him.

It was the English, too, I can see now, who in part determined our attempt—or "assault," as the true Alpinist
would put it: I like the term better, myself—on Monte
Rotondo. For we soon discovered that our little inn at Vizzavona was a favorite stopping place of theirs, especially
when they were contemplating a bit of a jaunt up the
mountain. It was their jumping-off place, so to speak, being
more or less at the base of it, and I suppose it was only natural for the proprietor, a chunky, barrel-chested man,
fiercely mustached but very agreeable, to assume that we
were there for the same purpose.

At first, Wynn and I were against it. We had done about
all the walking we wanted to do, on the horizontal plane,
and the thought of doing much more, and vertically at that,
didn't greatly attract us. But the inn, though small, was remarkably neat and cozy. And since we were there in early
summer, which put us off season, we had the whole place to
ourselves. When we sat down to dinner, alone in the tiny
dining room—with the wind sounding in the pines outside
and the feeling of mountains around us—it wasn't hard to
imagine that we were actually in an Alpine chalet, readying
for an adventure tomorrow. At any rate, over coffee, we
changed our minds.

We would go, we said, and instantly the proprietor took

us in charge. He'd have a lunch made for us, he said, and he'd have us waked early. The climb wasn't hard, and not dangerous. We wouldn't need guides, though if we had stopped in the village below they would probably have said we did, and have charged us accordingly. But there were some rough spots, and some viewpoints, too; he would map out a route for us over breakfast next morning. For Wynn and me, who had thought until then that to climb a mountain all you had to do was to keep going up-hill, it was a little dismaying.

Next morning, however, we were off—Wynn still with his cane. I had looked askance at it in Ajaccio, but had then said nothing. Now I ventured a mild protest. "With the cane?" I asked, and Wynn said, "Why not?" I had no immediate answer. Later on, as I've suggested, we were both extremely glad of it.

After all these years, I remember the climb only glancingly. Since then, luckily, I have done some climbing, or walking, in the Alps, and as I look back on the Corsican adventure I realize that in its way it was a replica, in miniature, of a real Alpine ascent. There was the same easy start, and the same feeling of continuousness, through the pine woods at first, the ground sloping gently upward, and then out on the upland pastures, the fields starred with spring flowers and full of cows newly loosed from their wintering in the barns in the village. After that the ground grew steeper. Meadowland gave way to rock, and the going got rougher. We went on; but, as I say, I don't remember the climb in detail. There was one place, though—the proprietor had warned us about it, as I recall, and told us how to avoid it, but apparently we'd lost our way—when we found ourselves in a slanting wilderness of huge boulders, as if a rockslide had come to rest, piled up in a narrow ravine, and we had to worm our way through the massed obstacles, or climb over them. Soon after that, snow appeared.

It was only in patches at first, on the north side of the rocks or the ridges, where it had lain since the previous winter. But the sight of it was strangely exhilarating; we felt we were really in high country at last, and the chill of the air added to the feeling. Higher still, the snow became continuous. The mountain terrain was getting steadily steeper, too. It was fluted with rough, spiny ridges of rock, running down from the summit. But the gorges or ravines between were all filled with snow, hard-packed and granular from the alternate thawing and freezing—corn snow, as I know now, it would be called by a skier—and a little dirty from its long exposure. But it was snow still, all the same! We felt wonderful; we were in the high altitudes at last.

We were working our way up the snowcap; we were well on our way along it when—well, I don't know precisely how it happened. Wynn, possibly, slipped and planted his walking stick a little more firmly into the snow than he'd done before; perhaps the crust here was thinner than elsewhere. At any rate, the cane not only went in, it went all the way in, and so suddenly that Wynn, not expecting such an outcome, lost hold of it. It went right on down through, and as it did, a section of the crust a foot or so in diameter gave way, too. We peered down through the aperture; what we saw—and heard as well as saw—was a gulf of blackness, emptiness, with, far down at the bottom of it, forty or fifty feet below, a glint of light on wet rocks and the sound of water running.

As I've said, there were ridges of rock running up either side of the snow. I don't know how Wynn got over to the nearer one; I lost sight of him for a few moments. For that matter, I don't recall clearly how I got over, either; all I know is that we both landed there, intact, and a little breathless—and then settled down to review the situation. What had happened, of course, was that we'd been traveling along blithely on what's called a snow bridge, and a snow bridge, I've since learned, is a fairly common and dangerous phenomenon in the warmer seasons, when the snow melts and runs off underneath, melting still more snow as it goes, until only the hard, frozen crust remains. But for us, the effect was as startling as if a piece of flooring in a fifth-story apartment had given way, revealing the basement below, or a section of a real bridge had dropped off as we were midway of it—and we regarded all the snow around us with great distrust from then on.

There was still the mountain to be climbed, however. The top of it—if it was the top; it could well have been a shoulder obscuring the real summit—loomed only a few hundred yards above us, and the ridge leading up to it, though rough and at times precipitous, looked as if it could be conquered. We might have conquered it, too; in fact, we were readying for the final dash when we discovered that somehow, in the confusion of getting off that snow slope, we had lost our lunch.

It was a good lunch, too, or it had been; we knew that because the proprietor at the inn had shown it to us, to prove that he wasn't stinting us, before doing it up in a neat package and depositing it on our table ready for the rucksack at breakfast—a plentiful supply of sandwiches, as I remember, cheese, radishes, and, to top it off, a bottle of wine. It was gone now, though, still sliding down the slope probably, if it hadn't hit rocks and started bouncing, and technically it was Wynn who had lost it, since it was he who had been carrying the rucksack at the moment. I couldn't blame him, though, for it's more than likely that if it had been in my hands I'd have dropped it, too. The thing now was to take stock of the situation and make plans for future action. I'm afraid we decided the latter part of the problem rather summarily.

I don't know what the veteran mountaineers would have done in such a situation. After all, they have guides and porters and so on, and camps set up and stocked with provisions all along the way ahead of them. Above all, they don't make mistakes. I'd read time and again, in Alpine literature, that you *can't* make a mistake in mountaineering: if you do, it is likely to be your last. Well, this wasn't our last in the sense intended, for we survived it. But it was the last one we made on Monte Rotondo. The descent from the position achieved, as the Alpinists put it, was made in slightly more than two hours, and, though I can't be sure, I believe it may have been a record for the route. We'd not only been thoroughly scared; we were hungry.

As I've said, though, we survived, and as a matter of fact I made an even more difficult climb with another painter friend of mine, Julian Levi, a little later, up the rue Monsieur le Prince, in Paris. Ordinarily, the ascent is not an arduous undertaking. The rue Monsieur le Prince runs from the Odéon to the Boulevard Saint-Michel, and ordinarily its gradient is scarcely perceptible. But as anyone who has tackled the high peaks can tell you, conditions can vary radically, according to the time and the circumstances in which an ascent is attempted. In this instance, Julian and I arrived at the base, or the Odéon end of the street, at around 4:00 A.M., after an extended trek through the bars and cafés in the region of the Halles Centrales, and as I recall, we were heading, vaguely, for a boîte near the Place

Saint-Michel called the Bolée de Cidre, which we hoped, being run by a Norman, would still be open. (The Normans, in my experience, never stop drinking.) At such times, though, the negotiation of practically any street can have its problems; indeed, they all seem to slant a little, and when we came upon a length of rope among some building materials piled along the sidewalk, we considered it to be only the part of prudence to borrow it and rope up for the difficult terrain ahead. We had hardly started on our way again when a group of four or five girls came out of a house across the way.

The rue Monsieur le Prince had—at that time, anyway—an oddly mixed sort of tenantry. It was about equally divided between excellent old rare-book shops and, as the phrase goes, houses of ill fame, and it was obviously from one of the latter that the girls had emerged, for, as was the custom in those less inhibited days, it had some such name as "Au Panier Fleuri" blazoned on the door, and considerable floral embellishments painted across the façade. The girls now were on their way home, however. They had finished their day's, or night's toil, and I imagine no group of women could be found in all Paris who were less interested in carnality than they were at the moment.

They were interested in us, though, and with some reason, since the times could hardly have been many when they had come out on the street at such an hour to find it the scene of an Alpine foray. And they were buxom, high-spirited girls, I remember, young mostly, and some with the bloom of the country still on them. (It occurs to me now that the Paniér Fleuri may have had its Norman affiliations, too.) At any rate, they simply pounced on us, questioning, chattering, laughing, and then running alongside and around us as, still enjoying our exploit, we plodded solemnly on our way. In a sense, one of my fondest and most vivid memories of all those days in Paris is the scene as I recall it that night: the narrow, ancient street with its shut façades, gently curving, gently ascending, and lit as much by the chill predawn illumination as by the street lamps; and the girls in their light summer dresses—for the moment, as innocent as children in their delight and excitement—dancing along beside us all the way to the Boulevard Saint-Michel.

 thirteen

I must be one of the very few people who ever carried a canoe across a good part of Normandy; indeed, at the time I'm speaking of—the early nineteen-twenties—there were very few people in France who ever *had* a canoe, in the first place. It wasn't until a few years later, and then rather cautiously, that the French began toying with the idea of canoeing as a part of the *vie sportive*. In that earlier day, a canoe was regarded exclusively as one of the appurtenances of the American Indian, and nothing for any sane white man to monkey with.

The canoe in this instance didn't belong to me, either. It belonged to a friend of mine named Jim Butler, who lived in a little Seine-side town called Giverny, about fifty miles downriver from Paris, where I spent a couple of delightful years, working desultorily on a novel, when I was fresh out of college. It was with him, and in it, that I made the trip I've just referred to—which, incidentally, turned out to be one of the strangest journeys I've ever made, as well as one of the most arduous.

That last is odd, for I've always ranked canoeing, along with bicycling, as one of the easiest and pleasantest possible means of self-propulsion. Walking is all right, but it's slow, and it can be disheartening, too, when, as often happens—particularly in France, where even the secondary roads are laid out with military precision—you come over a rise fairly early in the morning and see your whole day laid out before you in a straight line across the valley beyond.

In addition to a rowboat's being so heavy and unwieldy, you can't even see where you're going in the darn thing. But with a canoe, as with a bicycle, you get full return for the effort expended. You get your money's worth, so to speak, in both ease and responsiveness, and when Jim suggested, early one summer, that we make a combined canoeing and camping trip up through the interior of Normandy, I was delighted.

I couldn't have asked for a better companion. Jim was the son of an American artist who had come to France in his own youth and had settled in Giverny—then one of the headquarters of the Impressionist movement—and Jim, a painter himself, actually had spent the larger part of his life there. Yet, curiously, he had a good many purely American traits and predilections. Tall and rangy-looking, he was a great outdoorsman, which most Frenchmen at that time most definitely were not, while in the canoe (which, as I recall, he'd had to send all the way to the States for) he was as much at home as an Indian.

He and I had made other, shorter excursions: down the Seine to the locks near Les Andelys; up the Epte, the swift little stream that flowed into the Seine not far from Giverny itself; or just paddling about in the maze of winding channels that threaded the miniature delta at the confluence of the two.

This excursion, though, was to be more ambitious. The Epte flowed down from the center of Normandy, some seventy kilometers or so to the north of us, and Jim had noted, looking at a map one day, that another stream, the Andelle, which entered the Seine a fair distance farther downstream, had its source not far from that of the Epte.

The three, then, made a sort of rough triangle, and one that seemed just made for a canoe trip. We'd go down the Seine from Giverny to the mouth of the Andelle; up the Andelle to its headwaters; across from there to the Epte (it looked like a fairly short carry, on the map); and then, gaily, down the Epte to the Seine and Giverny. We figured a total distance of about two hundred and fifty kilometers, or roughly one hundred and fifty miles, for the trip—five easy days in a canoe—and except for the trip up the Andelle, it would all be downstream.

So we packed our camping equipment—I had just a ground sheet and a couple of blankets and a rucksack, but I was younger than I am now, and hardier, and they'd served me well enough on other occasions; Jim's was only slightly more elaborate—and, early one bright morning, we started off.

The map we had consulted was a sectional one, for motorists, and it didn't actually show the headwaters of the Epte and the Andelle; the two streams ran off the top of it in thin blue threads, apparently just before they reached their sources. But that didn't bother us; from the looks of things, the streams should come still closer together farther on.

And it didn't bother us, either, to discover, when we were well on our way, that between us we'd somehow neglected to bring the map along; after all, you can hardly get lost on a river, and in a way I suppose it even added a little spice to the adventure, made it seem more of a pioneering exploit, done on our own. But those two things were to be our undoing later.

We didn't know that then, of course, and certainly all the earlier part of the journey was practically pure delight. To be sure, it was stiff going for a while, when we started up the Andelle, but we had expected that. The Seine Valley, in the part we were in, alternates between chalky limestone cliffs and sloping hillsides—all of them outposts of the great Normandy Plain that stretches out to the north, plateau-like, beyond them—and any river, such as the Andelle, entering the valley from that side, has a fairly steep drop to make before reaching the Seine's level.

So though the Andelle wasn't torrential, exactly, it was consistently swift, and we had to paddle hard for some hours—and at times even get out and carry, past small rapids—before, with almost startling suddenness, we emerged on the plain itself. All this, however, was on the second day, and the trip down the Seine, on the first, had been wonderful.

The Seine isn't fast, but like all great rivers it is powerful. Not so broad as the Mississippi (though from the low vantage point of a canoe it almost seems so), it also moves in a series of great looping curves, carrying its brimming load of tugs, barges, and other traffic with it, and there was something almost exultant in the feeling of being swept along in that busy procession, riding the same current if not at the same speed, while on either side, on the banks, the little towns slipped by, alternating with the pale, gray-white cliffs and the green, sloping farmland.

We had decided not to try to do any cooking. As I'd learned on a walking trip to Italy, earlier, camping out, at that time, was still a little suspect in France. Fundamentally, the French simply couldn't see why any sensible per-

son should *want* to go to such lengths to make himself uncomfortable. They connected it with tramps, tinkers, gypsies, and similar riffraff, and we knew that if, in addition,
we lit fires, we would probably have the whole countryside
down on us.

So we stopped here and there for our meals, or a drink
or two in between, at the towns along the way or the occasional fishermen's cafés we found at the riverside. But I
don't want to go into too much detail, and anyway all that
part of the trip comes back to me only glancingly, in little
separate episodes.

I remember a stretch, in the middle reaches of the Andelle, where we traveled for hours through a mighty forest
—the Forêt de Lyons, a state forest, of course, with the
trees as perfectly aligned and as immaculately tended as all
such are, but otherwise as somber and darkly impressive as
the wilderness. We traveled late that day, I remember. Our
practice was to stop fairly early for dinner at some town,
and then paddle on till we found a quiet camping place.

This time, though, the passage through the forest had
delayed us, and we did our last paddling at precisely that
final, precious hour of twilight that the French anglers
most prize. The Andelle was lined with fishermen, all standing prayerfully silent along the banks, with their lines in
the stream, and though we went past as stealthily as we
could (Jim was a fisherman himself), we came in for a
steady series of angry looks and muttered curses, all the
same. We spoiled a lot of men's fishing *that* day, all right—
but what else could we have done?

Once, too, we came to a place where the Andelle trav-
ersed a large estate—some very wealthy man's shooting
box, no doubt—and a low wire fence had been strung
across the stream, more or less barring it. We ducked under

easily, only to be hailed soon after by a guard or game-
keeper, complete with Norfolk jacket, puttees, and shotgun, who ordered us off. We argued spiritedly (for it was
obvious that to make a carry all the way around an estate
of that size would be a fearful undertaking), our position
being that it made no difference who owned the land, the
waters themselves, everywhere, were public property. I
don't know who was right, really, about that. But there
seemed to be a certain logic in our position, and the French
are a logical people. In the end, the guard gave in. He
waved us on. But the French—and the Norman French,
especially—are suspicious, too, and he took the precaution
of marching along the bank beside us, his shotgun at the
ready, all the while we were passing through the property.
It's the only time I've ever had an armed guard on a canoeing expedition.

Then, there were all the lovely little towns that we
passed: Fleury-sur-Andelle, with an ancient fountain in the
square; Périers, in the midst of the forest; and Elbeuf-sur-
Andelle, where the café proprietor, despite his corduroy
pants and espadrilles, turned out to be an American, from
Brooklyn. (He was an Army veteran who had married a
French girl and settled down.) Forges-les-Eaux, once a
popular watering place but now grim and deserted, was
farther up, and it was not far from there that the stream
had run off our map. It was only a little beyond this point
that we began to run into difficulties.

What we discovered—and even this not immediately—
was that we hadn't taken fully into account the fact that
our map was a road map. In other words, it had been drawn
up with motorists in mind, not canoeists, and, in consequence, though the roads and highways had been rep-

resented accurately, the courses of smaller streams, like the Andelle and the Epte, had been largely guessed at.

Most particularly, whoever had drawn our section had continued the line of both beyond the point where either one bore any resemblance to a river at all. We had barely left Forges-les-Eaux, and were still well short of the place where we'd thought we'd be starting our carry, when the Andelle dropped to the size of a rivulet, and soon after that to a trickle. We were scraping bottom constantly, and in the end we were forced to concede that the canoeing part of our journey was over; the time for land travel had come.

The question was—travel where, and in what direction? We didn't know, and, it turned out, no one else did, either. There was no language difficulty. Jim's French, of course, was fluent, and mine was good enough so that I was usually taken for a Belgian—no compliment, except linguistically, for the French at that time hated their "little allies" to the north, but still it gave me a certain Continental feeling. I was flattered. No, the trouble was that we were in real back country there, in the heart of Normandy—the land flat and rather barren, the towns isolated, the inhabitants poor, mostly, and indrawn.

Except for an occasional visit to the nearest market town, they had never been anywhere, really. They just didn't *know* where the Epte was, and, in a way, they had no reason to, for, as we later found, the Epte—the real Epte, at the point where it was big enough to be recognizable as a river—was a good forty or fifty kilometers south of where we'd seen the last of it on that map. Up where we were, it was probably only a rivulet, unnamed and unnoticed— one among many others running, apparently at random, through the fields.

I say "probably" because it wasn't till two days later,

and much farther down, that we finally located it. Meanwhile, we walked. We had caused great interest before, among the washerwomen along the riverbanks and in the towns and cafés we'd stopped at. To guard against theft, or just mischief, we had always carried the canoe and our packs along with us when we went ashore for a meal, and crowds had always gathered, staring silently at first, and then edging forward to question us about our canoe.

They knew vaguely that it had something to do with the *Peaux-Rouges*—the Indians. But for the most part, they found it impossible to believe that so frail and small a craft could carry two men, and they invariably followed us down to the landing or the riverbank to see us off.

Once, indeed, in a village whose name I forget, the mayor of the place came down, too. He was a typical Norman— stout, rugged, and ruddy, wide-hatted and heavy-booted— and, exercising his official prerogative (and before we could stop him), he stepped right down into the canoe, flat-footed, just after we had put it into the water. It flipped him instantly, of course, and though he wasn't hurt when we dragged him out, he was undeniably wet, and we left that town in a hurry.

Now, though waterless, we were even more of a cynosure, trudging through that sun-baked region, in and out of villages where no boat, probably, and certainly no canoe, had ever been seen before, stopping here and there to ask for a nonexistent river. People must have thought—and, I'm prepared to admit, with good reason—that we were lunatics.

For our part, there were times when we thought that they were. I can see now that it must have been the canoe, more than anything else, that confused them. We carried it upside down, in the conventional fashion, single file, one man forward and the other aft, with our packs slung over our backs, and it must have been something of a surprise to the passer-by to see such a strange four-legged contraption approach him, and then to have it hail him.

"*Monsieur, connaissez-vous un fleuve, une petite rivière, qui s'appelle l'Epte?*" one of us might say, and he'd stop and stare at us.

"*Comment?*" he'd say, and the question would be repeated. But by now his eyes would be riveted irretrievably on the canoe.

"*L'Epte,*" Jim or I would say, trying to nudge him along mentally. "*Il se peut que c'est très petit de ce côté-çi. Mais ça descend à la Seine.*"

By this time, though, the passer-by's attention would be thoroughly divided and his mind confused, and when a Frenchman finds himself in this condition, he usually blames it on your own inadequacy with his language.

"*Comprends pas,*" he would invariably say, shaking his head, and hurry on his way.

Meanwhile, as I say, we walked. Carrying a canoe isn't bad if the carry isn't too long and (more especially) if you know where you are going. But this was developing into what must have been the longest carry in all French history, and as for its direction, about all we could do was to head generally east and south, which was where we knew the Epte *must* be, and leave the rest to luck. Under such circumstances, the weight of a canoe combined with that of a rucksack can mount surprisingly.

I think the low point came on the second morning, when we woke to find a truck driver staring at us. We had camped by the roadside, of course—where else was there? —but had retreated modestly behind a hedgerow to do it. The hedge hadn't been high enough to conceal us from anybody on the seat of a truck, however, and now here the truck driver was, in the chill morning light, staring down at us in frank amazement.

"*Nom de Dieu, qu'est-ce que c'est que ça?*" he demanded, pointing at the canoe.

We told him, and then, hastily seizing this new opportunity (for he was a cocky-looking fellow, obviously a city type and hence, presumably a well-traveled man), we added our query about the Epte.

"The Epte? What's that?"

"A river."

"A river!" he cried, and suddenly he burst out laughing. "You've got a boat, and now you're looking for a river to put it in! Seems to me you should have started the other way around!"

In the end, we stumbled on the Epte ourselves, but once we did, the postman helped considerably. We found it along about noon of the second day of our tramping, and at the point where we came on it, it was a fairly meager-looking little watercourse. But it did look, somehow, purposeful.

It was bridged where the road crossed it, and the bridges looked old and well established; and since it meandered a good deal—again, a sign of an old stream—the road crossed it a lot. And it was headed more or less in the right direction. But it was still far too shallow to support a canoe with our weight added—all it would support was the canoe alone, with our rucksacks piled in it—and we were cautious. Earlier in the course of our carry, thinking we'd found the Epte, we'd got started down what must have been the Béthune, and might well have landed in the English Channel if we hadn't got worried about the direction it was taking us, and hadn't yelled out to a woman doing her washing on the riverbank, and if she (wiser than most of her neighbors) hadn't yelled back, *"Non, non! Ça va à la mer!"*

We had had to backtrack then, so now we were taking no chances. Yet the chance to get the canoe and our baggage into the water and off our shoulders was far too attractive to resist. So we decided, for the time being, to divide forces—I taking to the road to make inquiries as I went along, and Jim wading alongside the canoe and waiting for my report at each place the road crossed the stream.

It was an emergency measure if there ever was one. But fortunately it turned out successfully, for about the first person I met was the postman I mentioned a while ago, making his deliveries and going the same way I was. He, too, was a typical Norman, with his uniform cap, brass-buttoned blue coat, ruddy face, and fierce mustache, and he had no more idea than anyone else that we'd met so far what the name of the stream was.

But some sense of official obligation seemed to stir in him, or maybe it was simply that the problem fascinated him. Anyway, he took charge of me at once. "We'll find out. Don't you worry about that, young fellow. You just come along with me. This road follows it for quite a way. We'll find out," he told me—and it was only then, because of a kind of owlish solemnity in his manner as he said it, that I realized he was fairly drunk.

That, in a way, was an attribute of his calling. The Norman, dour, cranky, and suspicious as he is, nevertheless has a tradition of hospitality, and one of its tenets is that any visitor, particularly one doing him a service, such as bringing him a letter, must be welcomed with a drink. The drink is usually just a small shot of Calvados, poured straight from the bottle and tossed off neat, but the effect is cumulative.

The postman, clearly, had made a number of deliveries already, but he was used to Norman hospitality, and I wasn't. So, alcoholically, I soon caught up with him. We would stop at a farmhouse (in that region, many farmers live on their own property instead of in the villages, as is usual in the rest of France), and he'd deliver a letter or a newspaper, or a package. The bottle of Calvados would come out.

"Listen, my friend," the postman would ask. "That little brook across the fields there—how does it call itself? The Epte?"

We would be standing in the farmyard—in France, a rectangular area, with the house, the granary or barn, and the stables enclosing three sides of it, and a high iron gate against the road—and the place would be swarming with chickens and children, and the air thick with the mingled odors of cheese, wine, cookery, and manure. Invariably, there would be a chained police dog, snarling and snapping, in one corner of the yard, and, also invariably, the farmer, in his sabots and corduroys, would stare at us heavily.

"*Connais pas*," he'd say. "From what I know, it has no name. It's only"—and he'd shrug his shoulders—"the brook."

"But it goes to the Seine? My friend here is an American, making the tour of France in a canoe—*un canoë, mon vieux*, the same type of boat the redskins use—and he seeks its destination."

"*Connais pas*," the farmer would say.

And we would sweep on, delivering a letter here and a parcel there, and at the next bridge we'd find Jim waiting, as we had arranged. Jim, before long, had enough depth of water to travel in the canoe, instead of wading along beside it. By that time, my postman and I were arm in arm.

As I recall, it wasn't till after the third such meeting, and some five or six more shots of Calvados, that the postman and I met with success. We came to a farm more sizable than the others had been; the courtyard was cobblestone-paved instead of just mud, and it seems to me that there was even a brassbound old Renault touring car parked outside it. The farmer, for all his country clothes, was obviously a man of substance, and he had the brisk, confident air of a man who has voyaged widely, who has seen the world.

"If *he* doesn't know, no one will," the postman had told me as we approached the place. And sure enough, he did.

"*L'Epte? Bien sûr, c'est l'Epte!* You didn't know that, you?" the farmer said to the postman.

"I know it well," he went on, speaking now to me, in the manner of one well-traveled man to another. "And it's true. It descends to the Seine, and as it goes, it grows larger. There are narrows farther on, but at Gisors there is room even for barges, and when it reaches the Seine, the big river . . ."

But by now the postman had clapped me on the back and was shaking my hand.

"Well, my friend, your troubles are ended!" he cried. "You can go on with your hearts at ease." He turned to the farmer. "He—he and his friend in the canoe beyond . . ." he said, and paused for emphasis.

I had told the postman the simple story of Jim's and my adventure as we'd walked along the road. But I'd noticed already that it had been growing perceptibly in minor details as we'd gone along. Now it really bloomed. "They have come from America *en canöe, mon vieux.* They were making the tour of the world in that fashion, till they got lost here! And now, thanks to you, they can go on—to the Seine, to Paris, to everywhere!"

There was no point in contradicting him, and anyway his enthusiasm was contagious; I felt that if we could only get out of this benighted region, we really *could* go anywhere. Meanwhile, though, the farmer was eying me.

"Across the ocean?" he asked. After all, the Normans are a hardheaded people.

"Ah, no," I said.

"But across La Manche—the Channel?"

"Ah, yes!" the postman interposed.

He wasn't going to have his story spoiled, and I saw the farmer's hand move toward the bottle. It occurred to me that maybe that was where the postman had been urging it all along.

"That calls for something extra," the farmer said. "It is not every day that one encounters men like this."

Calvados, raw as it is, is powerful. I don't remember much about what happened after that. The postman and I made our way to the canoe, somehow, and once Jim and I had got well on our way—down near Gisors, say—our route was through familiar territory, and so a bit anticlimactic. What I mostly recall is our last glimpse of the postman.

He was leaning on a bridge, watching us as we shoved off. "*Vivent les Peaux-Rouges!*" he yelled—and then, centering his sights a little, "*Vivent les Américains!*"

"*Vive la France!*" we yelled back, and dug our paddles in for a racing start. He was still standing there, waving—and weaving, a little—as we looked back from the first bend.

 fourteen

Even now, waking up of a dull morning, I can find pleasure and consolation by reminding myself that away off, some four thousand miles or so to the east of me, is Venice. Venice is still there, that incredible city; and if I were only in the same room I occupied when I was there a couple of years ago, I might go to the window and (already hearing the soft, continuous, somehow plaintive-sounding lap-lap-lapping of the little waves against the building wall outside), pull those heavy, metallic Venetian curtains aside, and see again the dancing flash and sparkle of the sunlight on the constantly gently moving waters of the Grand Canal; see the traffic—a big *vaporetto*, perhaps, coming up swiftly and passing, its passengers spaced along the deck in languid Italian attitudes and its wake setting rocking a couple of double-oared working gondolas, plodding more slowly, their long slim hulls loaded with merchandise and the oarsmen at stem and stern leaning, twisting, returning in rhythmic unison—and see, too, again, the tight-crowded, tall-windowed, and pillared, ancient façades of the palaces lining the Canal's other side.

I suppose everyone who has ever been in Venice carries

pictures like that in his mind forever after. But mine seem especially vivid, for I missed seeing Venice when I was first in Italy, many years ago, and with the passage of time I was beginning latterly to feel that maybe I never *would* get there, and my memory of it now is therefore all the more prized. I was lucky in this instance, but that hasn't always been the case; indeed, I seem to have a penchant for missing places—always, of course, on the carefree assumption that I'll get there next time I'm in the general region. I missed seeing the Grand Canyon when I was out West once, years ago: I wasn't really very far from there, but I'd just got bored with traveling. I missed New Orleans by inches, too, on another trip, and there must have been a dozen other times when I've turned back, foolishly, just short of the goal.

I missed Venice, however, because of a quite different set of reasons—involving, among other considerations, the editors of *Broom* (one of the so-called "little magazines" of the twenties), and the banking practices in Europe of the same period. *Broom*, although it had started in France, was then being published in Rome, and it enters my story for the simple reason that it owed me money. This was for a couple of short stories I'd sold the magazine, and it wasn't a large sum—around a hundred dollars, as I recall. I had no fear, either, that I wouldn't get paid for them in due course, for *Broom*'s editor was a wealthy young fellow named Harold Loeb, himself a writer, and, unlike a good many other little magazines of that day, it was completely —indeed, magnificently—solvent. It was just that in the spur-of-the-moment way we all lived in those times it occurred to me that if I were to go down to Rome and collect the money there, I could use it to help finance a little trip

through the rest of Italy—and so get all the good of it, so
to speak, at once.

So, though Venice was even then my principal destination, Rome became, for financial reasons, my primary one.
I planned to walk most of the way, at least as far as Marseille, and sleep out, too, whenever it was possible.

But I didn't intend that to include the cities I might
go through. I had no intention, for instance, of trudging
for a whole day or more through Paris, with my rucksack
and blanket roll on my shoulders, before getting beyond
the city's multiple suburbs. I took the train instead, down
as far as Sens, some hundred kilometers to the south, had a
look at the town, with its solid old early-Gothic cathedral,
and started walking. Almost instantly—French provincial
towns are so compact—I was in open country. I was on my
way.

I woke next morning to find the country not so open
as I'd thought when I'd camped the night before—and that
involves the one aspect of my little expedition that was at
all disagreeable. Perhaps unnecessarily, I must pause here
to note that French farm life is very different from ours.
Only rarely there does a farmer live on his actual farm site;
he lives in his village, has his grange and his stable there,
and commutes, so to speak, each day to the fields he plans
to work, ordinarily in a ponderous procession consisting
of a high two-wheeled farm wagon or two, horse-drawn
and loaded with implements, such cattle as he has, guarded
by a boy or girl with a switch, and followed by his sons or
hired workmen, if he has any, on bicycles.

The custom dates from feudal times, when the village, in
the shadow of the castle above, offered the only safe refuge,
and certainly it has helped preserve that peculiarly cozy

mixture of close community feeling and pure rusticity that one finds in a French farming village.

It has its disadvantages for the casual camper-out, however, as I discovered next morning, when I woke up early—and how early!—to see a couple of burly Frenchmen, dressed in sabots, corduroy pants, and jerseys, and armed, if my memory doesn't exaggerate, with pitchforks, staring down at me, while, just over my head, it seemed, a huge draft horse chewed its bit and stamped a hoof impatiently. I had eaten my dinner in the first town I came to outside Sens and walked on again, and the big, quiet field, nicely hedged away from the road, had seemed miles away from any hint of humanity. So it had been, then. But it wasn't so now, and the pair above me, obviously its owners, looked definitely unfriendly.

At least the older one did. He was a stockily built man, I remember, with brown eyes and a big mustache, and he had the brisk, authoritative air of a man of consequence in his own community. The other, a somewhat taller, gawky youth whom I took to be his son, mostly grinned uncertainly. It was papa who conducted the interview.

"*Qu'est-ce vous faites ici, nom de Dieu?*" he demanded, in a broad, rolling, country accent. "*D'ou est-ce que vous venez?*"

"*De Paris, monsieur,*" I told him placatively. "*Et je fais du camping seulement.*" This was a term just achieving currency in Paris, where *la vie sportive* was beginning to attract the younger generation, and a lot of Anglicisms, like "knockout" and "knockouter," "sailboating," and so on, were enriching the French language in consequence. I gave the word the proper pronunciation, too, with the accent hard on the "ing," but in spite of that it was meaningless to him.

"*Comment? Vous faites quoi?*" he asked, obviously puzzled, and I decided to drop that line right there.

"*Je fais un petit voyage à pied,*" I said, reaching for a simpler level of expression, and when he demanded where to, I said, "Rome." At this, the farmer stared at me.

"*A Rome,*" he repeated, and glanced at his son. The son was still grinning. "*Et vous allez toujours à pied?*"

I just nodded. Somehow, I had already sensed that the wind was turning in my direction. And so, it turned out, it was. For one thing, I must have been a puzzler to the man from the start. And at that time, too, the French felt basically that a man had to have a pretty good reason to want to walk anywhere, if he could afford to ride. At any rate, when he spoke again, it was with a curious mixture of interest and solemnity.

"*C'est—pardon, monsieur,*" he said, with a certain cautious respect. "*Mais je vais vous demander. C'est à dire . . . ce que vous faites, c'est une espéce de pélérinage?*"

I hadn't quite thought of it that way, till then. But it was an awkward moment all round, and I had to get out of it some way. Rome, too, is Rome, and it has many facets of attraction; I hope the Church will forgive me if I allowed my cultural pilgrimage to be colored a little by spiritual considerations. And I didn't actually say yes, or no. I just bowed my head gravely—and from then on nothing was too good for me.

There was a little brook they pointed out to me at the foot of the meadow where I could wash up, and they hovered over me while I did it; they even tried to force part of their lunch supply on me—consisting, as I recall, of plentiful amounts of cheese, wine, onions, and a big loaf of bread. I refused. As a matter of fact, I'd had a ham sandwich made up for me at the restaurant where I'd eaten the night before, as a kind of provisory, or prebreakfast, breakfast. But I decided not to wait there to eat that, either. To tell the truth, I was afraid that if I lingered too long they might get to questioning me about my pilgrimage, and it might be embarrassing. There are times when a good, speedy exit is indicated, and this seemed to be one of them; as it was, I left with handshakes, hearty good wishes, and hand-wavings all round, down the road.

But it had been unsettling, and I realized that under the circumstances I would have to change my routine a little: what I did from then on was to break my camp and get up and out before even the farmers were stirring, and let breakfast wait till I'd covered the five or six kilometers to the next village farther on. By that time, of course, I'd be ravenous, and my hunger would certainly not be dimin-ished when I smelled the rich smells of fresh country bread, oven-toasted, and of *café au lait,* prepared in the true coun-try fashion, with the coffee cooked right in the milk, rich, thick, and powerful—as these were set before me on the terrace of some tiny café I'd fallen on, on the way. Oh! those lazy, luxurious, leisurely breakfasts I had, sitting alone looking out on the cobblestoned village square, with its pump or fountain in the middle; the sun still low in the sky and the air cool, but already beginning to vibrate with the promise of heat; and the town, with the men departed to the fields, settling down to its placid, housewifely daytime procedures—of steps being scrubbed, bedroom windows being opened and the bedding hung out over the sills to air, while all up and down the Grand' Rue the shutters were clattering up on the *boulangerie,* the *épicerie,* the *char-cuterie,* and the first women shoppers were coming past, black-bloused, black-skirted, white-aproned, and with their eyes cast discreetly sidewise on the oddly clad, puzzling stranger.

Indeed, oh! the whole trip! Though I hadn't fully realized it, I had chosen one of the heartiest, most hospitable parts of France for my adventure—the section down through the Burgundy wine country into the Midi—and I think my reception, weird and fantastic as I must have seemed to the people there (a rich American, and *walking*) was more easygoing than it might have been if I'd chosen a dourer region, like Normandy, for my expedition. As it was, I think one of the nicest things that ever happened to me anywhere happened at Nuits-St. Georges (as a village, hardly more than a row of high-sided, stuccoed houses set against a steep, chalky hillside, as I recall it, and yet, as a name, how evocative to the wine lover), where I'd stopped around noontime for a bite at the local café and, not feeling especially hungry, had just ordered some bread and cheese and a glass of wine—and was surprised instead to be served a beautifully light, fluffy omelette, accompanied by a fresh green salad and fried potatoes.

"*Mange ça, mon petit,*" the *patronne* told me. She was a big, red-cheeked woman, not old, but solid and powerfully built; she had every right to tutoyer me, as if I were a child. She, too, apparently, believed that no sane person walked if he could afford to ride. "*Je sais ce que c'est d'avoir faim. Ça te fera du bien.*" Behind her, an older woman, standing in the door of the kitchen—her mother, probably, and the fabricator of the omelette—nodded and smiled encouragingly. I ate the omelette gratefully, but I had the feeling, as I'd had in the field outside Sens, that I was being coddled a bit more than I deserved.

Otherwise, the whole trip presents itself to me now as a kind of slow unrolling of gently sloping countryside, the roads chalk-white and blazing where the sun hit them, but generally tree-lined and also generally free of all but the most desultory traffic; and with always, whenever I topped the rise from one valley to another, a little town waiting in the hollow below, its church tower rising staunchly above the huddle of houses surrounding it.

And against this, as the background, there are the little separate incidents, inconsequential in themselves but somehow memorable; the time, for instance, down near Macon, when I found myself walking between twin hedges of blackberry bushes, the berries full ripe but, because the French have no liking for them, disregarded, and I walked along, literally stripping them off by handfuls and eating them as I went; the two or three days when, leaving the highways, I followed the Saône-et-Rhone Canal, walking along the towpaths and stopping at the tough little bars that stood at every lock; the time, at Chalon-sur-Saône I think it was, when, the weather looking unfavorable, I put up for the night at a roadside inn and found myself almost literally transported back at least a couple of centuries in time. "Loge a Pied et a Cheval," a faded sign said, which was what had attracted me; the place was packed with farmers and drovers, come in for the next day's market; we all ate at a long common table in a big room on the second floor, and there the bedrooms were, too, ranged along a U-shaped balcony overlooking the inn yard and the stables below. It was the sort of inn yard into which d'Artagnan might have ridden, or—the heavy iron gates on the fourth side thrown wide—a ducal coach might have been driven, on its way from Dijon to Paris and the Court.

As so often happens, too, one of my vividest recollections is also a completely isolated one. It was a wide starry night, somewhere—and I can't even remember where, now

—along my journey, and I had made my camp on a little knoll, overlooking a narrow valley. I was smoking a last cigarette before turning in when suddenly a train came thundering up on what I immediately realized was a railway line in the valley and went past with a roar and a rush of glittering windows. I had no way of knowing, of course, but I was instantly convinced that it was the famous "Train Bleu," headed south for the Riviera, and I had for a moment that possibly childish but exquisite pleasure of seeing without being seen, of watching, unwatched, from my lonely little hillside. I was going to the Riviera, too, and even farther, though no one on that crowded train knew it!

I'm still far from explaining why I didn't get to Venice. That, however, was the product of a long series of circumstances, but the first warning, as I see it now, was sounded one day when I'd stopped over at Lyon—if it wasn't, possibly, even earlier. At any rate, I guess the real moral of my whole tale is no more than a confirmation of the ancient axiom that man is a gregarious animal. He seeks the company of his own kind, and when deprived of it, certain psychological changes are likely to set in. I'd been two weeks and more on the road by then, alone, bedding late, rising early, and moving on furtively from field to field. It had been fun, too, from one point of view; it had been an adventure. But from another, I was living the life of an outcast, a pariah, and somewhere along the way (maybe even that night when I saw the train go by) the second point of view, the lonely one, had begun to supersede the other. This had happened, too, without my realizing it— till it was brought home to me that day in Lyon.

Oddly, too, I was then metamorphosed, relatively at least, into a man of fashion, for on leaving Paris I had shipped a suitcase ahead to Lyon, and now, having caught up with it, I'd put up at a good hotel, had a decent bath and a general cleanup, and settled down for a few days of just not walking. It was on the second day, as I remember, when the incident happened, and it was simple enough, superficially. I was passing through one of the public squares when I happened to see a couple of beggars washing up in the pool around a fountain there. They were really ragged creatures; but for all that, in France, as in Italy, where the street life goes on more unashamedly, it was a fairly common sight. They themselves, moreover, were quite careless of my own or of anyone else's stares; in fact, obviously, they were relishing this chance for a cleanup. My own identification, however, was instant and complete, and I find it hard to describe the feeling of both kinship and revulsion I felt for them.

It was not linked so much to what I had been, or had done, or even what I would do; it was more a kind of omen, a suggestion of what I might be led to do, given the circumstances. And somehow, it settled my walking trip, right there. I didn't even have to think about the matter further; I just knew, then and there, that this phase of my Italian expedition was over. I had planned to walk farther, perhaps even as far as Avignon, and stop there for some sight seeing. But I was now far too impatient even to pause there; when I left Lyon, it was by train, and my ticket was for Marseille, direct.

For the matter of that, I now had something else to worry about. This was in the deepest sense financial, and it was because, before leaving Paris, I had done what all my friends assured me was a woefully foolish thing. To be brief about it, I'd drawn six thousand francs from my bank, which in those days was ample for the trip. (And in Rome, don't forget, there were a hundred dollars or so, more, waiting for me.) But even I could see that it would be foolish for me to carry so large a sum on my person in the way I was planning to travel. So, spurning bank drafts and other such paraphernalia, I just held out some two or three thousand francs to take with me and mailed the rest in an envelope, addressed to myself, General Delivery, Marseille.

This, on the face of it, I suppose, was a foolish thing to do, and my friends in the Montparnasse quarter, in Paris, had said so, in chorus. To be sure, the ordinary practices of easy credit, so common nowadays—the Diners' Club card, the gasoline service coupon, and so on, not to mention the traveler's check—were still pretty much unknown then. Cash was what was expected, and cash was what one usually dealt in. Still, my Montparnasse friends said, I'd been rash.

"Don't you know that's the way the French post-office people make a living?" they told me. "They *take* the money. They do it as a matter of course, and then tell you the letter must have been lost, or something. Boy! You'll never see *that* letter again!"

I'd pooh-poohed all this at the time. But I was a little taken aback just the same, and when I got to Marseille I checked in at the nearest hotel, barely paused to dump my suitcase and rucksack, and hurried on down to the main post office. Looking back, I see the rest as a series of movie fade-ins and fade-outs, beginning with the post-office clerk at Marseille.

I can see him still, in his light yellow working smock, yawning as he reached up for a sheaf of letters, pigeonholed above, riffling through them and shaking his head, reaching up for another pack, riffling partway and—it was then that my heart started beating again—handing out my precious letter, intact, to me.

We fade out on him, fade in on the brisk young clerk,

brush-mustached, neatly cravated, at the British bank I
went to a few days later, when I was getting ready to leave
Marseille. The barbs of admonition sink deep, and though
I'd done all right with my home-made way of getting
money to Marseille, I was now afraid to trust it further. A
proper bank draft was what I wanted, and the bank clerk
was only too glad to oblige. Yes, indeed, he could fit me out,
he told me. As it happened, his own bank had no branch
in Rome, itself. But it had what was called a "correspondence" with an Italian bank, the Bank of Milan, which did
have, and under the terms of the correspondence, each
bank honored the other's commercial paper. He made out
the bank draft for me then and there.

We fade again to Rome. I can also still see the face of
the bank clerk there—round, brown-eyed, wispily mustached, the brow furrowed with quick Italian sympathy—
as he told me that it would be a good ten days before the
draft could be cashed and I could get my money. This was
not the Bank of Milan; it was the bank where *Broom* kept
its account, and I had been taken there by a man named
Edward Storer, the associate editor of the magazine, because, as far as he and I could discover, no Roman branch
of the Bank of Milan existed. The clerk at *Broom*'s bank,
sorrowfully, confirmed this. It was *incredibile*, he said that
the *Inglese* at Marseille hadn't known about it, but the fact
was that Milan had closed its office in Rome some months
earlier; and under the banking practices then existing, it
would be necessary for my poor little draft to be sent to
Milan, stamped, verified, certified, and whatever there, and
returned to Rome—when, and only when, it would be
cashable.

He'd be glad to handle the whole transaction for me, he
said. Meanwhile, I had learned from Storer that Harold

Loeb, the owner and editor in chief of *Broom* was in Berlin, on a short vacation—and Storer, a large, very British, rather ponderous fellow, had no authority in Loeb's absence to make any payments to contributors at all. I had about a thousand lire in cash in my pockets, and it may have occurred to me about then that, just possibly, I'd have been better advised to stick to the mails, in transporting money.

About the best thing I can say of the period that followed is that if a person is going to be broke, Rome then was one of the nicest places to be broke in. I wasn't really *broke* broke, of course. I had a thousand lire to get me through the ten days ahead. That meant one hundred lire a day, or rather less than two dollars; and this, allowing for my hotel charges—a not extravagant, but still irreducible, item— was even then just about the practicable minimum. But I adhered to the daily allotment rigidly; it made, at least, for a highly simplified schedule.

I had my breakfast at a little *cremeria* in the quarter, worked a while in my room, and then went out to wander. Rome, then, in those pre-motor-scooter, pre-motorbus, even largely pre-motorcar days, was a city of quietness. It was a leisurely city, too, small, compact, and still pretty much contained within its circular wall. But, above all, it was *quiet*, and almost all my recollections of it then are interlaced with the humbler, homelier sounds of every- day, nonmechanical existence: one heard horses' hoofs and the rattle of carts and carriages on the cobbled streets as much as one did motors; in the squares one heard, uninter- rupted by any other noises, the plash and splash of the Roman fountains; and there was a spot I early discovered called Tasso's Seat—a bench in the crook of an ancient oak, on the side of the Janiculum Hill overlooking the Trastevere quarter, to which the poet was supposed to have come to meditate—where I could not only look down into the clutter of streets and houses below me, but could actually hear the occasional sound of voices, rising: children playing or a mother calling to them, and the intermittent cries of street vendors.

I'd have lunched en route, so to speak—on ripe figs, ripe olives, grapes, pickled white beans, and so on, all served up in paper cornucopias by the street vendors and topped off, perhaps, by a couple of those crisp little Italian doughnuts and an *espresso*, taken in some workingman's *caffe*. And, as I was discovering, being more or less on the loose, as I was, often brings you into contact with some wonderfully odd and interesting people. There was a slight, shy, permanently sad-faced Italian Army officer, retired, whom I struck up an acquaintance with at a little restaurant off the Piazza Nettuno that I frequented, evenings, largely because it may well have been the cheapest restaurant in Rome. It was called, I believe, the Trattoria Nettuno, but it was usually referred to as Pina's or Giuseppina's, after the daughter of the proprietor, and it had a certain random bohemian atmosphere all its own. Among the other habitués were a couple of Italian journalists who usually sat talking darkly together in a corner; a red-faced, rather mysterious cleric, a German, who was engaged in some special studies (he never divulged what) at one of the institutes in the Vatican; an Irish ex-boxer, a former lightweight named "Ping" Byrne, lath-thin, white-haired, and sixtyish, who had wound up, improbably, as a boxing impressario in Rome; and, occasionally, Storer, the *Broom* editor I mentioned earlier.

Storer, when he came, was usually accompanied by a couple of other *Broom* writers, on their way through Rome. Byrne, invariably, had an entourage of Italian fighters, large, earnest, pacific young fellows—and the combination was a lively one, especially when, with the kitchen closed, the curtains drawn a little to discourage outsiders, and the wine flowing, we settled down to make a night of it. Pina's was a tiny place, half wine shop and half restaurant really, bare brown-walled, with the wines in big barrels ranged along one side and a few tables along the other, and perhaps its very compactness made for conviviality. I remember one night particularly when Ping decided, despite his age, to favor us with an Irish jig.

This, it must be said, happened not infrequently with him. But that night, for some reason, a kind of dancing craze took hold of us. Even the journalists mellowed, and performed a tarantella; I demonstrated the Charleston, while a couple of the boxers did a sort of Italian version of a Cossack dance—in the end, with the tables pushed back, we all joined in a crazy reel, with Pina herself being whirled, not unwillingly, from one partner to another.

All in all, then, the Roman episode had been fun; so it seemed at the time, and so it seems now, too, in retrospect. When it ended, however, it ended suddenly. As it happened, my bank draft came back from Milan a day or so ahead of schedule, and I cashed it; and Harold Loeb arrived from Berlin at almost the same time, and he was both quick with payment and disarmingly apologetic about the delay. There I was, then, suddenly transformed from poverty to affluence, from rags to riches. I was loaded with money, I was foot-loose again, and now all Italy lay ahead of me; I could start out any time I wanted to for the hill towns (everyone had told me I simply *had* to see them) for Bologna, even for Venice. . . .

What I did was something quite different, and it proves not only that one man's pleasure can be another's pain; the same ambivalence can exist in the individual himself. For again—as at Lyon—the balance had been shifting, the point of view changing, and it wasn't till I had all that money in hand that I realized it. In another mood, those handsome thousand-lire notes could have have meant reassurance, and a means to further wandering; in my mood of the moment, they meant simply escape. I threw a farewell party at Pina's for everyone, and next morning I was on a train headed straight back to Paris. Venice could wait. Right now, I wanted to get to some place where I *knew* people, and people knew me.

 fifteen

I began this book in random fashion, and I might as well end it so. How else, indeed, end a volume about a life that—thank Heaven—has not ended yet? In my own case, at any rate, I find myself left with a lot of odds and ends, too scattered for any attempt at continuity, and too tenuous for other than glancing treatment.

I had started a chapter on lentils, for example, and their influence on my development. This was considerable, since, as I look back on it now, lentils helped a good deal to get me started as a writer. I lived on lentils—plus a few oddments—for a whole summer in Woodstock, New York, back around the beginnings of the nineteen-twenties. I had sold a story for fifty dollars, with which I hoped somehow to get through the summer. Someone had told me that lentils were a complete food, satisfying every dietary requirement, and with the whole-hog-or-nothing trustingness of youth, I invested in a whole hundred-pound sack of them; once committed, I had to see the thing through. So I ate them doggedly, unremittingly, and it turned out to be a turning point, for if I hadn't had a girl who *refused* to eat lentils as assiduously as I did, and if my father hadn't dropped in unexpectedly on one of his trips back east, and been faced with lentils, too—well, who knows what might have happened?

But I gave up halfway through the chapter, because a feeling of tedium seemed to be creeping into the recital. Lentils, Lord knows—and despite the fact that there exists a Hindu saying to the effect that "Rice is good, but lentils are my life!"—are not only a monotonous diet; they introduce a certain monotony into one's whole life as well.

In a sense, they take your life over. Cooking them is only a part of the problems they present. They must be cooked for an hour or more. But before that they must be soaked for at least twelve hours, or overnight, in order to get the real goodness out of them. And before *that*, the batch to be soaked, and boiled, must be spread out scatteredly on some flat surface and picked over carefully. For lentils, growing close to the ground, have a marvelous affinity for other small objects—pebbles, pellets of clay, curled-up leaves, and so on—of similar size and coloration; and though I don't know how sorting is done nowadays, though I suspect it may be electronically, in my day it was of the essence to weed out such tiny intruders with the utmost diligence, if you didn't want to crack a tooth or get a mouthful of clay later on.

I did the sorting on the top of a kitchen table, in a one-room shack I'd been lucky enough to rent, cheap, for the summer; and there were times when—with one batch of lentils bubbling away on the kerosene stove, another soaking, and still another spread out for me to pore over—I felt surrounded by lentils! As I say, when I started writing about them, I felt something of the same overpowering omnipresence of the damned things was getting into the story.

But I can still see my father, sitting opposite me at my kitchen table, looking first at the dish of lentils I had set before him and then at me. He had arrived, as I've said, unexpectedly, just as I was sitting down to dinner, and the least I could do was to ask him to join me. There was a bit of luck there, too, for me, by the way, for if he had got there earlier he would certainly have taken *me* out to dinner; I'd have been too shamefaced to mention my curious diet, and—well, again, things might have turned out differently.

As it was, I had done my best to rise to the occasion. There is one good thing about lentils: You can add almost anything to them, from potatoes or onions to sliced frankfurters and leftover meats, and it is invariably an improvement; and as I recall, I had doctored the dish up lavishly with whatever oddments of that sort I had in my larder. Lentils, though, are still lentils, and my father, fortunately, liked good eating. Finding me in that little shack, with that kind of food before me, must have been, to him, much as if he had found me living as a squatter in the desert or had arrived just in time to rescue me from a Bowery bread line.

"You really mean it, don't you, boy," he asked finally, "about this writing business?"

"Yes, Father, I do," I said, and he thought some more.

"Well, I'll have to speak to your mother about this," he said at last, almost sternly. I knew what he meant, though. My father never did anything official, concerning me, without consulting my mother first. But I could tell what was in his mind; and already, dimly inside me, I could smell salt waves, feel the heave of a deck, and see Europe in the offing.

Later on, with the lentils set gently aside, we discussed the matter tentatively over a somewhat better meal at Mrs.

Allen's home restaurant, at that period one of Woodstock's best eateries.

I had thought, too, to do something about that first ocean crossing, surely an important event for any twenty-odd-year-old fellow, especially in those days before jet planes and intercontinental missiles. I sailed on a vessel called the *Oropesa*, and I'm afraid both it and the flag it sailed under, that of the Royal Mail Steamship Company, have now vanished. The year was 1921, well before the time of "tourist cabin." I traveled third class, or steerage, and it was really that: we slept four to a minuscule cabin, in bunks, and ate at long tables, passing platters of food companionably along the length of them; and except for a couple of English younger sons, homeward bound after a go at sheep farming in Australia, and myself, our complement was all European, peasants mostly, and with a preponderance of Germans among them.

Yet it was all new to me, and hence exciting; it was fun besides, for after we had been under way for a day or two and got shaken down a bit, we found out that we had the wherewithal for a good deal of cheerful festivity amongst us. An Italian got out an accordion and another one sang; someone else produced a harmonica, and a pair of Hungarians did some rousing dances. Before you knew it, we had a sort of combined concert and *fête maritime* going on almost every evening on our little semicircular deck space, and such gay ones that people from the first and second classes began trying to infiltrate us. For the most part, we cold-shouldered them.

The German contingent stayed aloof from all this. In effect, they cold-shouldered us, and it wasn't till nearly the end of the voyage that I discovered why, and also why there was such a solid little group of them. It was, I've always thought, a curious story. For these, it turned out in the end, were people caught midway—through no fault of their own, and though they themselves didn't even know it at the time—in the disastrous fall of the German mark, in that decade after World War I.

They, too, were farm people, all elderly and all from the same region of central Minnesota, and they showed a remarkable solidarity—which led me to feel that some enterprising travel agent out there had booked passage for them all together.

And they'd been immigrants once, and had homesteaded probably; and had farmed, and been saving, saving, saving for an eventual return to the homeland. They'd been pitting their hard-earned dollars, as they accumulated, against their value in German marks. And then the value of the mark had begun dipping a little, from the traditional five to the dollar down to ten, then to fifty, a hundred.

It was easy to see how it must have affected them. It was too good a chance to be missed, for now a man could figure his capital, in marks, at twenty or more times what it had represented before! It was a windfall, a bonanza, and the thing to do was to take advantage of it at once, for it was clear that the fall must be only temporary; all their faith in the power and authority of even a defeated Germany forbade any other conclusion.

So they had sold their farms and totted up their savings. They had turned their money into marks, and it was easy, too, to see why they looked down on us. Most of them were dressed in farm clothes still—the men in gum boots and mackinaws, the women full-skirted and either shawled or wearing their menfolks' discarded fur caps—but that didn't matter. New clothes could wait till they got nearer home again.

The truth was, they were rich! It wasn't till the last few days of the voyage that a kind of collective tremor went through them. The sad fact was that the mark was still falling. We didn't get individual copies of the ship's paper in third class, but a copy was posted daily on a bulletin board in the mess hall, and more and more as the days went by one could see them clustered in front of it, studying the exchange quotations and watching the mark's now accelerated descent.

At first the mood was mainly rueful, like that of a gambler who discovers that if he had only waited a while he could have run an already sizable take even higher. But it was mixed with apprehension, even then, and when we ran into storms and the crossing was stretched out from ten days to eleven and then twelve, one could feel their dismay and apprehension growing. These were simple people, really, and paper money has its alchemies more mysterious than gold. But even they were beginning to realize that the same fortunate tide that had lifted them up was now, inexplicably, running against them.

At the time, I felt little sympathy for them. They were a hard-bitten lot, as I recall them, heavy-featured and heavy-humored, suspicious and at the same time overbearing, and I was too young, I suppose, to appreciate how great a part the rough, grinding life they had led—the prairie isolation, the penny-pinching; the still-greater isolation during the war years, no doubt—must have played in forcing them into that mold.

But later on, in France, as I watched the *chute* of the mark, I often found myself wondering what had happened to them. Looking up the figures recently, I found that while the mark stood at around two hundred at the period when I saw them, it had dropped a year later to eight thousand to the dollar, and a year after that to around forty thousand. It ended at over four billion—by which time, of course, or long before it, all their years of work and their momentary wealth had shrunk to the value of an instant and the profit of a penny. Having two Yankee parents, I'd been brought up to have a healthy respect for the "value of money." Now I'd had at first hand an illustration—and how dramatic a one!—of how capricious that value can sometimes be.

But I was bent on getting to Paris, as I am now in this book, and there is so much still in between. Most beguiling of all, to me, are those winking little moments of pure remembrance, welling up from the deep past unexpectedly and bursting like bubbles, frail but luminous, obliterating the present.

I am walking up Lexington Avenue, late, past the Hotel Lexington (and a party of rosy-cheeked suburbanites standing under the white-lit marquee, their spirits slowly drooping but with their necks still draped in their paper leis from the hotel's Hawaiian Room: if they took them off, it would really mean the party was over): suddenly, I am not there.

I am walking along the rue Lafayette in Paris, and the Lord alone knows why, for the rue Lafayette, from the Trinité on east at any rate, is a wide, rather commonplace, workaday street, lined with small shops and inconsequential enterprises, running straight as a die out to join the Avenue Jean Jaurès at the Place de la Villette: a street unheroic, unhistoric, and certainly unpicturesque—and, as far as I know, nothing memorable ever happened to me

anywhere along the length of it to make it recur so frequently in my recollection.

I think it may be its very lack of picturesqueness that is
responsible: that, and the fact that I discovered it myself,
so it became my unique possession. It was so removed in
all respects from the "quaint," the touristy part of Paris;
and it led me to explore other areas of the city that were
equally workaday, equally humdrum—the region around
the Place d'Italie (where the Métro plunges earthward
after its perilous aerial flight across the Seine); Menilmon-
tant (and the young girl who wanted "*trois tunes*"); Pantin
(and the steamy, screeching railroad yards, and the little
Van Gogh-like bridges across the Ourcq Canal). These
were regions that no one I knew visited but myself. They
became in a sense my private property; while the glimpses
they gave of the everyday working life that went on behind the midtown façade gave a new dimension to my concept of the city.

Or (it is summer and I am in the country; I am trellising
my tomato vines) I find myself in the Raspail station of the
Nord-Sud subway: the station almost empty in the be-
tween-hours, and the high, arching, dirty-white, tiled ceil-
ing echoing with the distant rumblings and the vast, heavy,
rubbery breathing of the two tubes at either end. And
where was I going? Why?

There are mornings in New York, around ten o'clock
of a frosty overcast day, when the greasy-gray light, the
damp, keen-edged air, and some sudden concatenation of
sounds—unnoticed in themselves—remind me almost
achingly of Paris. (And I crossing the Pont-Neuf; a little
tugboat, all brass and varnished mahogany, just dipping

its black stack beneath me, as I head toward the rue Dauphine.)

Or it's night, and the home-hurrying passers-by trot-trot-trotting, shuttling from dark to light and then dark again, past the dimly lit windows of the little neighborhood shops along the rue Daguerre. . . .

The long, bleak *quai* of the Halle aux Vins; and ("the expectant autobuses rustling with hooded plumage in the trees") the little, dozing Place de la Contrescarpe; the tall, vaulted aisles of (Delaunay's) Church of Saint-Severin; and the gold-spangled, blue-ceilinged porch of Saint Germain de l'Auxerrois . . .

There are so many places that I revisit in Paris, or that revisit me. And the question is: Where do these exact, instant memories come from, and why? But wasn't it Einstein who solved a problem in physics, or whose mind solved it for him, while listening to a concert in Carnegie Hall? And who was the man—a psychologist, wasn't it?—who saw all the parts of an intricate theory he had been working on fall into place, as if of themselves, as he was stepping onto a streetcar in Vienna?

It may be a mark of passive acquiescence on my part, or a sign of justified, if smug, satisfaction (I incline to the latter view), but I'm convinced that the nineteen-twenties was a happier, more hopeful and confident time than we are likely to see again in many, many years. Every age, every generation, in its youth, has its problems, its trials, its triumphs, and its uncertainties. We had ours. But apart from this, ours had also the glorious feeling that we were truly on the threshold of a Golden Age.

We had it on the highest authority that the last great

war, the War to End Wars, had been fought, and we believed it. Not only we, but a good share of our elders believed it, too, and I can still recall the outcries of horror and shocked condemnation that swept the world when Laurence Stallings published that massive compilation of war photographs, around 1925, and titled it *The First World War*.

"First World War," indeed! To be sure, there was fighting going on here and there, sporadically: in the Riff, against Abd El Krim; and there were mysterious doings in Russia; the Japanese were beginning to throw their weight around in Manchuria. But that there would ever be another Great War, that was unthinkable; surely, stupid and tendentious as man naturally was, he must still have learned his lesson about that!

Stallings was right, of course, and already there were forces slowly gaining strength and direction that would eventually justify his ironic prediction. But I won't go into them here, for we didn't know about them. The young men of my generation looked forward to peace, to peace timeless, unhurried, and indestructible; I would suggest that you pause for a moment, as I sometimes do, to think about that, and compare the basic outlook it suggests with the mixture of frustration, anxiety, and downright fear that lies in the back of every man's mind nowadays when he picks up his morning paper or turns on the radio.

This fact, too, I think, had a great deal to do with creating the atmosphere of the period—a mixture of optimism, enthusiasm, and intense, if occasionally disorganized, activity. It was a fine time to be young in, especially in Paris, for Paris was the dream city for us all, and as dream cities should be, it was a faraway, mystical, magical place as well. There were no quick means of transport then, no jet flights,

no transatlantic planes of any sort. The wild ocean lay between, emphasizing the distance; and I still have, as another
of my recurrent images, a memory of my first sight of the
shores of France, close and getting closer.

My little liner, the *Oropesa* merely hove to in the harbor
of Cherbourg, on the way to its home port at Southampton,
and we passengers bound for France were ferried to shore
by a lighter. I was standing in the prow of the lighter; it
was dusk, but as we approached the landing I could make
out, first, the larger details, and then the lesser ones of the
scene before me: a battlemented fort, apparently ancient,
and a row of barracks nearby; beyond them—and all of
unfamiliar construction—the sheer, uncompromising,
stucco façades of the city's seaward-facing buildings; finally, a sort of promenade, along which I could see groups
and couples of people strolling.

Until then, I had been impatient for the landing. But
now, alone in the bow of the lighter, abandoned even by
the friendly little *Oropesa*, a kind of "moment of truth"
overcame me, and I can still recall the solemn feeling, not
so much of apprehension as of awe at my own temerity in
venturing so far afield, as I told myself, "All those people
are French. They all *talk* French. They are *French*."

But all that only added to the sense of excitement and
adventure. It was predominently a gay time, and it's no
accident, I think, that it was the Dada period—the one artistic movement I know of whose main purpose was having
fun. Montparnasse was the new Latin Quarter when I was
there, though Montmartre still had its adherents; and perhaps because of the devil-may-care atmosphere that Dada
induced, the quarter was full of amiable eccentrics.

There was a Polish painter who always wore cowboy
clothes, chaps, sombrero, spurs, and all; and a mum Nor-

wegian, tall, skinny, and death's-head pale, who dressed in a black frock coat and the black-ribboned stovepipe hat of the French professional mourners, and, like them, he professed to be mute. A kind of living *memento mori*, he would appear in a bar—say, the Dôme or the Rotonde, the two most popular Montparnesse cafés at the time—signal silently to the waiter for his glass of wine, drink it silently: the next time you looked, he would be gone.

There was a "baroness" of uncertain nationality who, anticipating the tactics of Gypsy Rose Lee, fastened all her clothing with pins, and often, as the evening wore on, would begin unpinning them; and there was an Englishman, Alastair Crowley, an avowed diabolist, who wore lace-trimmed shirts, velvet jackets, and occasional knee breeches, in a vague emulation of the Marquis de Sade.

But enough has already been written about the eccentrics of the period. They were the "fringe element," as one would say now, and, in general, an unimportant part of the scene. It was also the era of the "little magazines." *Gargoyle* was one of the earliest of these. Gotten out by a gallant couple named Arthur Moss and Florence Gilliam, his wife, it was strictly a hand-to-mouth, spur-of-the-moment venture; but, for all that, and for all its total lack of pretentiousness, it ran on for a respectable number of years and printed some remarkably fine stuff. *Broom,* published by Harold Loeb, a collateral member of the Guggenheim family, was more elaborate and infinitely more well-heeled; put out variously in France, Italy, Germany, and the Tyrol (it had a way of flitting), it was what might be called a "slick-paper" version of the little magazines, and it paid accordingly—as much as a hundred lire, or about two dollars, a page, for a story. (*Gargoyle,* as I recall, paid about fifty francs for a whole story, but the cheerfulness of the Mosses and the air of camaraderie they gave to the whole venture more than made up for the difference.) And then there were *transition* (spelled with a small "t" and put out by the Jolases, Eugene and Marie); *Secession;* Ford Madox Ford's *Transatlantic Review; This Quarter*—and intermittently and less dependable and long-lived, many others.

It was a crazy time, as I look back on it now, and in many ways, too, an incredibly innocent one, but, for all that, productive. Perhaps the best thing to say is that it was truly a period of experimentation. There was indeed a ferment in all the arts, and in the field of literature we had three titans leading the way—Gertrude Stein, James Joyce, and Ezra Pound—who in their separate fashions were manipulating the English language in ways that had never been done before; and if the headiness of all this made us sometimes a little punch-drunk or just plain silly, it must, I think, be conceded that we were honestly so.

Unlike the present "beat" generation, which sometimes seems to me to be playing both ends against the middle, we felt that if we were in revolt, we could neither give quarter to the enemy nor accept it. We were so far out, as the saying goes now, that success distressed us. Our "little" magazines remained determinedly little, eschewing anything so vulgar as wide circulations and financial profits; while a good review, if it came from one of the Pooh-Bahs of the period, was equally disturbing. I still remember that one of the French Dadaists, Louis Aragon—now, oddly enough, a leading figure in the Communist party over there, and presumably with no time for such nonsense—went so far as to write the book editors of the Paris papers individually, promising to horsewhip them if they so much as mentioned his new book. (Most of us had our parents to support us, of course—or to help, as mine did, while I earned a little money on the side—and the cost of living, owing to the exchange, was almost embarrassingly low. My average income, from all sources, was about seventy dollars a month, and I certainly never felt deprived.)

One wonderful thing about the nineteen-twenties in Paris, too, as I look back on them now, was that the "great ones," even the titans, were so accessible. You didn't have to make an appointment, and a pilgrimage, to meet Léger, Picasso, Satie, Pascin, Juan Gris, Tristan Tzara, or Brancusi, to mention a few names at random. You found them sitting at a table nearby in one of the cafés of the quarter, and as the evening wore on and mutual friends appeared, you were likely to find yourself sitting at the same table with them—or at their table infinitely rounded out, satellited, so to speak, with other tables—and talking and drinking with them without the least self-consciousness on either side.

Ford—now, it seems to me, one of the forgotten figures of the period, for both his influence and his generosity to younger writers were tremendous—was a great party-giver, often hiring a small café or a *bal musette*, complete with orchestra, for the purpose. (We had to chip in for the drinks, though, I remember, for in small matters like that he was curiously parsimonious.) So, too, though in different, more intimate fashions, were Pound and Brancusi, and at all their houses there was the same feeling of equality between the older and more-established artists and the young newcomers.

I believe I have said before that there was a certain bohemian atmosphere about the gold camps in the West; and, in a sense, in the Paris of those days, the same thing was true, for there, too, everyone was striving for new strikes or new discoveries—in the arts, this time, instead of in the ore lodes: anyone might strike it rich, and meanwhile there was room for all.

James Joyce was an exception, being more retiring, and so was Gertrude Stein, who just didn't like the randomness of café life. A big woman, calm, massive-faced, massive-bodied, with a brown Italian coloring that was accentuated by her habit of wearing loose-woven peasant-like skirts and blouses, and sandals, she lived with her life-long friend, Alice Toklas (smaller, wirier, and more active), in the famous apartment, 27 rue de Fleurus, off the Luxembourg Gardens, and in a sense presided there. I think now that she may have felt a certain frustration herself, for in her life-time she never got (has not got even now), the recognition that was due her for her influence in introducing an almost mathematical lucidity (the classic influence, as distinguished from Joyce's, the romantic influence), into the treatment of the English language.

At any rate, people came to her, not she to them—Sherwood Anderson, Thornton Wilder, Ernest Hemingway, among many others—and though a few of them, notably Hemingway, disavowed her later, I think most of us remember and treasure the warmth, the understanding, and (again) the genial feeling of artistic equality we got from her.

There are a couple of other random recollections that come back to my mind now and then; both are linked with that awed, trepidatory moment when I stood, at dusk (dusk, the coming of darkness as the shore grew nearer, are indissolubly a part of the remembrance), and realized that I was at last on the very verge of being plunged into a wholly strange country: France, the land of the French, the French language—French-dom, in short.

As a matter of fact, once there, I did better than I'd expected. I had had a considerable amount of school French, to begin with, which helped; and for another thing, I tried hard to fit in, I *worked* at it. It was somehow important to me not only to be in France and to speak French, but also as far as possible to *be* French; and I still remember the pride I felt the first time I really understood a remark in French without having to translate it first in my mind.

I was standing in a workman's bar down behind the Gare Montparnesse—a *zinc*, as they used to call it—and a little way down the length of it a couple of men in the hard-visored caps and leather jackets that many workingmen wore at the time were standing chatting over their glasses of red wine. Of the two, it is the one nearest me that I recall most clearly. He was short and chunkily built, with a cheerfully round, ruddy face and a huge sandy mustache, and it was he who made the remark that to me was magical.

"*Eh bien*," he said, as he lifted his glass. "*Tu sais, mon vieux, dans l'alcool il n'y a pas de microbes*"—and the soul-lifting thing, impossible to describe or to convey to anyone else, was that I got it, direct; it came through as naturally as if it had been spoken in English, without translation!

That was nothing, however, to the time I found myself *speaking* French without translation. I was walking along the rue de Rennes, near its crossing with the rue de Vaugirard; it was a clear, sunny day, and what traffic there was, was leisurely—when suddenly I saw a man stepping off the curb just ahead of me, and directly in the path of an oncoming autobus.

Without thinking, I yelled, "*Attention à la voiture!*"— and, just as the bus, its brakes screeching futilely, skidded past, he jumped back out of danger. He was one of those dapper, apple-cheeked, wax-complexioned Frenchmen, neatly barbared and tight with self-esteem, and from the glance he gave me, it almost seemed as if he blamed me for the blow to his aplomb.

I didn't care. He went his way; I went mine. But all the rest of that day, and for days thereafter, I repeated the episode in my mind.

"*Attention à la voiture!*" I had yelled to him; and I had done it without thinking, as naturally as if I'd been speaking English! I was a cosmopolite at last! I was in!

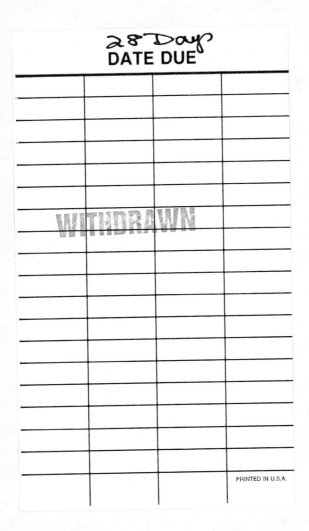

28 Days
DATE DUE

PRINTED IN U.S.A.